INDOOR CYCLING

The Accident-Free Aerobic Exercise

John Krausz and Vera van der Reis Krausz

Illustrated by Barbara Remington

Doubleday & Company, Inc.
Garden City, New York
1987

WARNING

Before making a drastic change in diet or exercise (if your doctor hasn't already suggested that you exercise) talk with your doctor about your health goals.

If you are under the care of a physician or a therapist for rehabilitation, discuss any recommendations we make before trying them.

If you have chest, neck or shoulder pains while exercising or shortly thereafter, don't just ignore them. If they don't go away in less than 5 minutes, see your doctor before you do another workout. If pain persists for more than 5 minutes, get immediate medical aid.

The most dangerous thing you can do is to end a workout with a sprint rather than a gradual 5 to 10 minute slacking off. If you have to get off to answer the phone before you can do a rolldown, stay active, swing your arms, jog gently or at least rock back and forth from leg to leg.

The dangers of not exercising are great. According to Dr. Per-Olof Astrand, one of the founders of the modern exercise movement, "A medical examination is more urgent for those who plan to remain inactive than for those who intend to get into good physical shape."

If you set realistic goals, indoor biking can turn your health around. The responsibility for your health is yours and your personal physician's. Any application of the recommendations set forth in the following pages is at your own discretion and risk.

INDOOR CYCLING

John Krausz and Vera van der Reis Krausz

Copyright © 1987, Two-Wheeler Books, Inc.

All Rights Reserved
Printed in the United States of America
First Edition

Library of Congress
Cataloging-in-Publication Data

Krausz, John.
Indoor cycling.
1. Exercise—Equipment and supplies.
2. Bicycles. 3. Cycling—Physiological aspects.
I. Krausz, Vera van der Reis.   II. Title.
GV543.K73   1987   613.7'028   86-11436
ISBN 0-385-27931-0

To Berenice Hoffman, our agent, and to Jim Fitzgerald, our favorite editor, who by a collective act of will made this book possible...to Satchel Paige, who suggested a sensible way through the aerobic madness of our times.

SATCHEL PAIGE'S RULES FOR RIGHT LIVING

Avoid fried foods which angry up the blood.

If your stomach disputes you, lie down
and pacify it with cooling thoughts.

Keep the juices flowing by jangling
around gently as you move.

Go very lightly on the vices such as carrying on
in society—the social ramble ain't restful.

Avoid running at all times.

Don't look back.

Something might be gaining on you.

EARLY HOME TRAINER.
This Buffalo home trainer (circa 1880) was advertised as the most complete on the market. It featured a cyclometer that rang a bell at every quarter mile and claimed to be adjustable to any leg length.

Table of Contents

INDOOR CYCLING

SPECIAL ADVANTAGES

- Circulates blood without shock to your bones or joints because the machine carries your weight.
- Shockless aerobic exercise—gentler on the joints than walking.
- Available every day—rain or shine—in the privacy of your home.
- Lets you avoid the danger of exercise class or running buddies' pushing or embarrassing you into overdoing.
- Controlled, measurable output.
- Greater range of leg movement than running or walking.
- Stretching is unnecessary for most people if they warm up and cool down enough.
- Lets you gain endurance for other sports that require special conditions.
- Lets you overcome injury without having to use a swimming pool.
- Reduces blood pressure and controls edema at a lower heart rate than jogging (this often lessens or even eliminates the need for blood pressure medication).
- No special clothes are needed. (This is often claimed by manufacturers, but you may be more comfortable in cycling clothes. Certainly firm shoes are a must.)
- Potentially, you can do it for a longer period of time than any other aerobic exercise.
- You can watch TV, read or listen to music as you get fit.
- Plus the advantages of any good aerobic program: weight control, stress reduction and protection against backaches, osteoporosis and all those middle-age problems.

THE USEFUL EXERCISE

There are about 20 million stationary bicycles sitting unused on sunporches and in basements, and another 1.4 million more were sold last year alone.

There are also 50 million or so seldom used 10-speeds sitting around that can be turned into state-of-the-art indoor exercising machines by the use of wind-load simulators (500,000 sold last year).

The stationary bicycle is the most common gym machine and the favorite instrument of exercise physiologists because it is easily calibrated and riding one is much less frightening than running on a treadmill.

Indoor cycling is the exercise of choice of injured runners and the one most prescribed by doctors and rehabilitation therapists because output can be constantly and objectively measured and monitored.

Because the weight of the body is supported by the machine, there is little pressure on the joints, making it particularly good for treating stress, obesity, chronic fatigue, arthritic and circulatory problems.

Elite runners use stationary bicycles for a second daily workout because they can cut mileage and avoid injury this way.

Unfortunately, the indoor bicycle shares with the outdoor one the idea that there is "nothing to it." Practically everyone makes the same mistakes: poor position, poor fit, overstressing the knees by pushing too hard against too high a resistance to get a "good workout," and setting unrealistic goals.

Almost anyone can gain aerobic endurance through indoor biking. If you use some sense and follow our suggestions, indoor biking should be injury free.

A lot of people bring a "last chance" attitude to exercise machines. Result: they often begin with a sense of desperation, which makes for rapid dropouts, just like the people who try to lose a lot of weight quickly.

But if you have started an exercise program and stopped, that doesn't mean you're a failure, it probably means you made a mistake in technique: doing too much too fast, or not doing anything because you don't have time for a full workout.

The exercise bicycle is a useful machine: it should help you get fit and lose fat. There must be some way for you to use it, if only to help you warm up for a cold walk—before taking the dog out, for example.

Available and weatherproof three hundred and sixty-five days of the year, you don't have to plan your life around your workouts.

Because indoor bicycling is injury free, because workouts can be easily controlled, you can train as hard as you want.

Long after the marathon runner has hung up his shoes the bicyclist can keep on pedaling.

Indoor cycling can be boring. All right, we'll admit flat out that it *is* boring. You've got to get through the first month.

It takes about a month for the body to adjust to something new, to build a new habit. After that, you will have found something to keep you amused while doing indoor biking—books, TV, daydreaming or listening to music. A while back Atari had a gizmo that linked a bike with a game computer, which gave us a whole new way to overdo it.

It's easy to overdo on a bike. When you get tired running or swimming you have to stop, or at least slow down. On a bike, a little coasting or a little letting up on the speed rests you enough so you can keep going, which means you can really beat yourself up on a bike because you can stay on it longer.

Set realistic long-term goals.

Rather than sit around, try to get on the bike every day, if only for a no-sweat 10-minute roll. If that's all you ever do—10 minutes five or six times a week—you won't gain much endurance, but after a year you will have turned some fat into muscle and lost several pounds, or at least not have gained your annual two to three pounds.

Everything that we suggest might not work for you. Coaches feel that they are lucky if their advice works for three out of four people. You have to build your workouts around what does work for you.

If you use your body messages, including your pulse rate, and some good sense, indoor cycling can help you achieve aerobic endurance with all its benefits.

Setting Realistic Goals

One of the main reasons for failure of any diet or exercise plan is our microwave thinking.

It took you years to get into this kind of shape, and your body has made all kinds of major and minor adjustments to help you adjust to a low level of activity. If you try to get fit too fast, you will produce exhaustion, listlessness, all the physical and psychological signs of overtraining.

Set goals for a minimum of three months; better yet, six months or a year.

The most important thing you can do in your first three months is to learn how to stay on the bike for 45 minutes.

You have to accept certain unpleasant realities:

Plateaus: times when you're stuck—you're not getting thinner or faster. If you don't accept the fact that your vitality ebbs and flows, a forced increase in training time or intensity is bound to produce both pain and overtraining effects.

Exercise can't undo it all. Some damage is permanent; narrowed arteries and veins may not widen (though auxiliaries may form); bones compressed by osteoporosis will not revert to their original shape; a liver injured by years of alcohol abuse may not cure itself.

For all its advantages, indoor cycling is not as intense aerobically as running on a treadmill or using rowing or skiing machines. As to how much longer it takes you to get the equivalent workout on a bike, the estimates vary from 10% to 25%.

Someone in good shape will become infuriated because they can't get over 80% of target rate on a stationary bicycle. A runner shouldn't expect to get much above 75% of capacity but can aim for much longer workouts.

So you pay for the safety and convenience by having to spend more. time. Workouts should be up to a third longer than the half hour three times a week that most people recommend; you don't have to increase the warmup or rolldown. The health experts who say half an hour three times a week are hoping you do 45 minutes anyway.

For the less fit, the problem is that they run out of leg strength before they have reached an aerobic level. Only 5 minutes of pedaling adds up to 250 repetitions. Leg strength builds fairly quickly, but for most people, it's going to take time to be able to cycle for 20 minutes without stopping.

BOREDOM

The world gets very small when it's just you pedaling away on your indoor bike, and it takes ingenuity and/or great inner resources not to feel like a kid waiting for the bell at the end of class.

Only the salespeople at the store would dare tell you that indoor biking won't be boring at times, so you have to prepare for this.

The catch is that the real improvements in health take a while to show themselves, and meanwhile you have to establish the habit of getting on the indoor bike. Psychologists say that it takes about a month for an adult to "set" a new daily habit.

To a certain extent, the more complicated the ritual, the deeper the habit will set. First you put on your rigid-soled shoes and change your clothes, then you put the cat in the other room, then you take a drink of water and get a towel to wipe off the sweat, then you get your clock facing front and the radio, tape player, TV or magazine ready...

You will have to find something besides the bike to keep you amused, because the long wild sprint inspired by a fit of boredom can tire you so much that it serves as an excuse to give yourself a day off, which can stretch into two and, before you know it, there goes your training program.

It can take as long as two months to really feel the training effect. Once you do, you'll be a lot more cheerful.

Let the Mind Drift, Let the Body Talk

The mind asks, "What's new?" and answers, "Nothing."

That's when we say we're bored.

The trick is to ask a bunch of new questions and try to pick up on all your body signals. You discover that you're pushing hard on the forward pedal, but only with the left leg, so you work on making the pressure more even. Your neck gets stiff and you stretch it or try out a new way of carrying the weight of the head.

Boredom is underloading. The isolation that any aerobic training gives you can allow ideas you've ignored to trickle up to the conscious level. Once you go aerobic and start to sweat a little, it is easy to let your mind drift. Some people just count the drops of sweat as they fall from their faces, others are content to watch the wavering needle go from 19mph to 20 and back. It can be a quiet, centering time when you have no other demands made on you, so you can truly rest your mind while working your body.

People who love biking outside find it particularly hard to accept the fact that the machine that keeps them constantly amused on the road can be such a drag in the house. Boredom is one reason bikers prefer rollers to stationary bikes...working on keeping your balance can keep you amused for quite a while.

Not an Immediate Problem

When you're just starting out, you should not be bored, or you're doing something wrong. You should be working on perfecting your position on the bike, getting your pedal revolutions up to 90 a minute, and finding out what it feels like to be at your proper training level.

If You Are Bored Immediately

You may be rebelling against the new stresses of sitting on the bike. You're angry that you've given yourself all this work to do. Calibrated stationary bicycles are the principal research tools of the work physiologists. In case you've forgotten, the "erg" is the basic unit of work, so they're not called ergometers (work-meters) for nothing.

There's a lot of the "last chance" psychology in taking on an aerobic exercise program. Five times

more people have tried running than there are runners. Many had to stop because of injury, and their limitations make them embarrassed, so some of the boredom is shame in disguise.

Some People's Solutions:

Serious Thought. Some people use the time they're exercising to analyze and start to solve problems they face at work or at home...or in serious abstract thought. And why not? All that extra oxygen reaching the brain should make you think better.

Peaceful Drifting. Some people find that indoor biking induces a meditative state, like yoga. You can let your mind drift, and problems you have been working on seem to solve themselves or seem much less important.

Unfortunately, until you have disciplined yourself to keeping a good cadence, drifting might make you slack off on the pedal revolutions.

Musical Accompaniment. A standby in exercise classes and company that many athletes can't do without, music makes exercise feel easier and time go faster. Eric Miller, a doctoral candidate in exercise physiology at Ohio State University, found that people who ran with music had lower perceived exertion and endorphin levels than when they ran without it, though lactic acid and heart rates were the same. "You can exercise at the same intensity, but do so with less effort," Miller concluded. Be sure to start and finish at a fairly slow tempo.

Television. The six o'clock news is many people's favorite; though a retired friend always cycles to two morning quiz shows.

Reading. Reading stands are available on many indoor cycles; there are also inexpensive ones that fit most handlebars. Gathering enough materials ahead of time is necessary; the small print in most paperback books is too hard to read. Library books and most magazines are ideal. Some people save the Sunday magazine sections for their training sessions.

Do it before you're really awake. Many people find that if indoor biking is part of the getting-up routine they've gotten it over with without having a chance to get bored. It's hard to replace the smug feeling that comes from having done something *that* good for you that early in the day. Of course, you can combine an early morning workout with any of the above suggestions that suit you.

Dr. Kenneth Cooper noted that people who set aside early morning time for their aerobic workouts were less likely to find excuses to stop after a few weeks. Recent data suggests that it might not be such a great idea, however: it seems that many heart attacks occur in the morning.

BIKE FIT

BIKE FIT AT A GLANCE

- Arm and leg length, not height, should determine fit.

- Hands should reach the handlebars without straining and with enough elbow room for easy breathing.

- Seat should be *high enough* to have leg straight (but knee unlocked) when foot is on the pedal.

- Seat should be *low enough* to pedal backward without rocking the hips.

- When the seat is moved up or down it also moves forward and backward.

- *Knees should never be in front of the center of the pedal.*

- Feet should be protected from pedaling forces with firm-soled shoes.

- Ball of foot, not the arch or the toes, should be on the pedal—and kept there with toe-clips.

- Each foot should have the same side-to-side angle as it does walking (don't try to restrain it at an unnatural angle).

Important Tips

- *Change the bike to fit you, don't adapt yourself to fit a bike.*

- *Never ignore knee pain:* check seat height, fore-and-aft position and foot angle: their correct placement are essential to protect your knees from injury.

- Once you have a good setup, give yourself about a week to get used to it.

- Don't expect the first setup to be perfect, but make further adjustments in very small ($1/8$th of an inch) increments.

- Check seat height every month or so—the seat may have moved or you may have stretched into a new, higher position.

- Wear the same shoes each time—changing sole thickness changes seat height.

- You might be lucky and fit on the saddle that comes with your bike, but don't count on it!

- A good bicycle store can provide you with what you need to make almost any bike fit you:

  Stems, handlebars, seat posts, pedals, toe-clips, and shoes.

  Padding for each of the places where you touch the bike: leather-covered foam-padded seats to fit wide- and narrow-spaced seat bones, chamois-lined shorts; foam-backed tape for handlebars that won't take regulation padding; Spenco hand pads, insoles and seat cover.

CONTACT POINTS

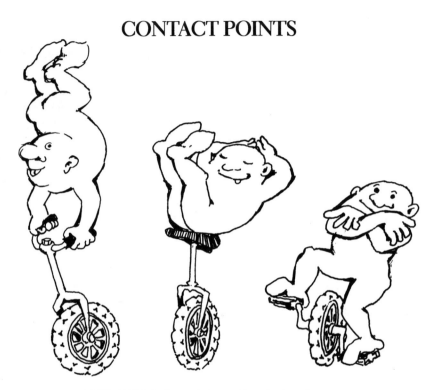

THE HANDS: In the upright position, the handle-bars should support most of the weight of the arms. In the more forward 10-speed position, the hands support up to about a third of the weight of the body.

THE SEAT supports the weight of the body, freeing the legs to spin the pedals.

THE FEET: The pedals support the weight of the legs so that the feet can turn the pedals freely.

BIKE FIT IN DETAIL

Even the cheapest regular bicycles come in different frame sizes. In contrast, most exercise bikes seem to be one-size-fits-all.

The bike should be adjusted to fit your body, not the other way around. Orthopedic problems have been caused by bad fit, especially having the seat too high, too low or too far forward.

Once you have approximated the correct position, give it at least a week before changing anything. Then change gradually, perhaps as little as 1⅛ inch (or millimeter) at a time.

Check your bike every month or so to make sure the seat height, knee and hand positions are still correct. As you become more fit, your tendons may stretch and you may want to try a more forward lean and a higher seat. Also, sometimes the seat clamp slips and the seat gets imperceptibly lower over a period of time.

We're talking fractions of inches here, not inches. One of the principles of adjustment is to try small changes and give yourself a few days to get used to them.

That does not mean riding with pain. Knee pain, in particular, is a red alert. Check to see whether your seat is high enough, then look down and see which way your foot is facing; perhaps it's been toeing in or out too much. Try changing the angle of your foot a bit and see if your knee still hurts.

An adjustment as small as a quarter of an inch may make an enormous difference in comfort after about a half hour of cycling. Since few people can stay on that long the first time, it makes sense to check the bike you intend to use very carefully to make sure it can be adjusted in all the ways you need to fit it to your body. Anyone whose body is not average—who has very long or very short legs or arms, or very wide or very narrow shoulders, for example—should be especially careful.

The Three Contact Points

The hands, the seat and the feet are the places where your body comes in contact with the bike. The ideal setup does not let you notice any of them while you are pedaling.

These three points of bike fit are interrelated, so that if you change one, the others may need some adjustment as well.

The Hands

You should neither have to stretch to reach the handlebars nor feel confined by having them too close to your body. It is hard to breathe properly while riding with the handlebars too close. But if

17

you have to strain to reach them, neck, shoulder, back and/or genital pain can occur.

On a regular bicycle, the stem that holds the handlebars comes in different lengths and degrees of up-and-down slant; it can also be raised and lowered about an inch. Most ergometers do not have these options but it may not matter since you sit upright.

HANDLEBAR PLACEMENT.
Be sure to leave yourself enough room on stationary bicycles whose front end can be adjusted forward and back.

The seat is on a rail and can be moved forward and back; but that is to position the knees correctly.

Upright position. You should be able to reach the handlebars from a comfortable upright position with your elbows bent but not squashed against the body.

Dropped position. A 10-speed on a wind simulator or rollers should let you reach the handlebars with about a 45-degree forward lean. (This is correct touring position; racing position is lower to minimize wind resistance.)

Women's handlebars should be level with the seat, men's about 2 inches below.

If the dropped handlebars put too much pressure on your hands, raise the handlebars further, tilt them up or replace them with straight bars. Use padded cycling gloves or Spenco's hand pads.

The Seat

There is as much variation in bottom size as there is in foot size—so there's no reason any one seat should fit everyone. Generally speaking, men's seat bones are closer together than women's, but there are some men with seat bones as far apart as some women's, and some women with seat bones as close together as a man's. A study of only 60 women showed a difference of 4 inches in distance between the seat bones! So some would be comfortable on a man's narrow

BACK POSITION.
Don't sit bolt upright. A slight forward position centers the weight over the hips better and helps avoid back pain.

saddle and others would need the widest women's.

What feels comfortable for five minutes can hurt a lot after an hour. Pressure and numbing from vibration can be unnoticeable for the first ten minutes and unbearable after a half hour.

Wide mattress-type saddles often have metal plates underneath which undo any cushioning effect; and the width can chafe the inner surface of the thighs.

Any padding effectively adds to the height of the saddle, which means you will have to readjust the seat height.

Sometimes a pressure problem in the crotch area can be cured by changing the angle of the seat. Men seem to be comfortable with it tilted up slightly, and women with it absolutely straight (tilting it down puts a lot of pressure on your hands).

If you have made all the adjustments possible on your machine and you are still not comfortable on the saddle that comes with the bike you have, take the seat and seat post to a good bike store and get a new seat that will fit the seat post.

The new leather-covered foam-padded "anatomical" seats and the chamois-padded bike shorts provide much better insulation than the old racing saddles. (The anatomical seats have hollows positioned to correspond with human pressure points. They come in men's and women's racing and touring models.)

19

Seat Height

The seat should be high enough to all but straighten the knee when the pedal is at the bottom of the stroke and the ball of the foot is on the pedal. The hips should not have to move from side to side as you pedal.

Have the seat low enough, however, so that you're not stretching to reach the pedal and can

SEAT HEIGHT.
Your leg should be almost straight with the knee not quite locked. With an average-size heel on the pedal, you should be able to pedal backward without moving your hips if the seat is at the right height.

keep the foot level with the heel down as much as possible. You should think of pedaling as moving forward rather than stamping down.

Sitting too low *or* too high is murder on the knees. When you are sitting too low your knee has to bend too much, which places too much pressure on the sides of the knee. When you are sitting too high, each time you straighten your leg the kneecap lifts free of the channel it usually rides in. It then thumps into place when you bend it, which is traumatic, especially since it doesn't always get back into the right groove.

Since a quarter inch can make a difference, wear shoes with the same sole thickness each time or you will have to change the seat height. If you pad the seat after you have set it up, you will have to lower it to make up for the extra thickness.

Many models of exercise bikes only permit inch changes in seat height because the seat post is adjusted by moving a pin from one hole to another, rather than by loosening or tightening a clamp. This does prevent slippage from one height to another but, unless one of the heights is perfect for you, be prepared to change seat post and seat rather than risk injury by riding with the seat too high or too low.

Horizontal Seat Position

When the pedals are horizontal—at three and nine o'clock—a plumb line should pass from the front of the knee through the axle of the pedal.

The knee should *never* be in front of the axle. If it is, the seat is too far forward, which makes the legs bend too much and puts too much pressure on the knees. If the seat is too far back the muscles are stressed, which is uncomfortable but less dangerous; older people sometimes prefer it this way: "It gives you more push."

So either put the bike with its side facing a mirror so you can see if the knee position is correct, or else have a friend or neighbor check it out.

When the seat is raised or lowered, it also goes backward and forward. By how much depends on the angle of the seat tube; this depends on the design of the exercise bike.

If two people with very different inseam lengths are to share a bike, two seat posts might be necessary, one with the saddle riding on a rail that lets you adjust the distance from the saddle to the handlebars. In any case, the same saddle or sad-

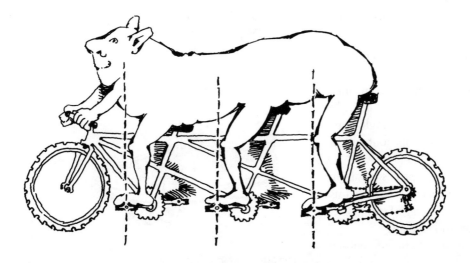

KNEE POSITION. The knee should not be in front of the ball of the foot when the pedal is at three o'clock—the most forward position. As the seat is raised, it goes back. Horizontal movement of the seat allows for finer adjustment.

21

dle tilt may not be comfortable for both people.

The Feet

The ball of the foot should be on the pedal, not the instep and not the toes.

Toeclips, cleats and straps will hold the foot in this position without strain, but it's important that they do not force the foot into an unnatural angle. Not everyone's foot naturally faces straight ahead, and if you try to force it to, you may get knee trouble.

Toeclips can be adjusted to point toward the bike or away from it by adding washers to the attaching bolts at one side or the other. There are also pedals available that tilt inward and outward and have built-on toeclips.

There is a limit to how much of an angle change is possible. If you toe in or toe out a lot you may not be able to follow the angle completely, in part because part of your foot will hit the crank.

It was possible to replace the pedals on all the exercise bikes we examined, so if you can't adjust the pedals to suit your feet, we suggest you replace them with rattrap pedals and toeclips.

Toeclips come in three sizes to fit different size shoes.

Leather-covered toeclips protect the shoe from being scuffed by the toeclip (they also move the foot back a little). Rubber bands or tape wrapped around the front of the toeclip will do the job.

If two people with very different size feet share the bike, get two-sided pedals and put toeclips and straps on each side. You might have to snug down the ones that aren't being used so they don't scrape the floor.

Shoes

Your feet contain 25% of the bones in your body, and during the forward part of the pedal

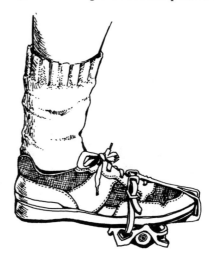

CORRECT FOOT POSITION.
The ball of the foot is over the axle of the pedal. The toeclip keeps the foot in this position. The shoe looks like a running shoe but is a cycling touring shoe with a rigid sole.

stroke the forces on the leg may equal the weight of your body.

The cycling shoe was developed to protect feet from these forces by distributing the pressure over the entire foot. How? By using a rigid sole made of wood, plastic or metal-reinforced leather. So we recommend, if not a cycling shoe, a stiff-soled tennis shoe or service oxford rather than a bouncy running shoe.

Certainly *not* riding barefoot. It might be all right for a warmup exercise, but you're not going to use the kind of pressure to go hard enough for a training effect—unless you're The Hulk.

Many people insert orthotics into their bike shoes. Spenco makes an inexpensive full-length liner or arch support that can serve for this purpose.

Because of the popularity of bicycling, touring shoes have been developed that you can walk around in even though they have stiff soles.

Some touring shoes have slots for the pedals to fit into. If these feel as if they are in the wrong place or at the wrong angle, fill the slots up with shoe goop or file them down with a medium-coarse metal file.

If you went out of your way to design a shoe that really isn't good for cycling, it would look like a jogging shoe: it's soggy and it's flexible; you have to compress it with each stroke. It might be all right for a casual bike ride or a 10-minute morning eye opener.

Like toeclips, once you've gotten used to stiff cycling shoes, you feel crippled if you ride an hour without them.

Of course, if you're light and you're flexible, you can get away with anything.

EQUIPMENT

OVERVIEW

We think that a moderately priced bicycle exerciser will do to get most people started on a program.

By the time you can go 20 to 30 minutes aerobically, you'll be strong enough to really test a more expensive machine. If you learn to use toe-clips and to pedal evenly, you might not need the additional sturdiness and precision.

If you're a record keeper, you'll be getting very useful information on an ergometer, since you'll be able to duplicate a workout.

An ergometer might be necessary for medical reasons. The sturdiness of a moderately priced ergometer could be a good investment in your health.

What bicycle riders have always wanted was to use a bike of their own on a stand as an indoor bicycle, with some means of creating resistance; this was provided by the wind-load simulators.

Riding a bike on rollers works well but takes a bit of learning. Rollers are great for developing leg speed and suppleness but they don't let you develop much strength unless a wind-load simulator is attached to the back of the bike.

Instruments for bikes will always be much cheaper than for ergometers because there are so many more bikes. They will also be much more easily updated. The electronic goodies that bike riders will be offered in the next few years boggle the mind. You're going to have bicycle computers that will communicate with personal computers and computerized wind-load machines that will increase the resistance according to a scenic videotape (climb the Rockies or join the Tour de France).

Wind-load simulators added to 10-speed bikes give you a larger choice of seat, hand and pedal adjustments than most ergometers or exercise bicycles. While they aren't as sturdy and they vibrate more, they are a much better buy, even if the bike never leaves the house except to go to the bike store to be serviced and have parts changed.

Machines to Avoid

Don't get exercise bicycles that fold, have frameworks on which you pedal one spring (or hydraulic cylinder) against another, or on which resistance is produced by turning a bolt against the crank axle. *All these machines can bite and may be dangerous to use, as are worn-out or poorly maintained bicycle-rowing machines.*

We don't recommend any machine that combines rowing and bicycling. While it might be good for a short intense workout, you're not going to want to stay on it long enough to get any aerobic effect.

Maintenance

Stationary bicycles and ergometers have to be serviced and lubricated to continue to work well. Good machines come with manuals that will show you just what to do. Checking through a bike repair book will tell you most of what you have to know. Caution, the resistance calibration on most good ergometers requires special tools and gauges to make the proper adjustments.

Be sure to set the resistance on your machine at zero when you're done with your workout. This will keep the cables and springs from stretching and throwing the machine out of adjustment. With machines that use a strap or large brake pads to create resistance, the wheel will freeze as the strap gets glued to it. This will happen when the machine is unused for a while. By resetting the tension at zero you will be able to peel the strap or brake pad off; often there is a deposit of goo that will have to be scraped off.

BEWARE OF THE BIKES AT THE GYM

Bikes in gyms get heavy use. Very often they are broken or poorly maintained. Take a very long warmup and decide if the one you're on feels all right before continuing.

"They're always broken," is the most common thing said about indoor cycles by "gym rats."

The high-tech gadgets on some very expensive gym machines (from $2500 to $20,000) are all totally useless to you if you don't fit comfortably on them. And don't let all those dials or fancy readouts trick you into overdoing.

The resistance adjuster is usually turned very high and sometimes sweat has welded it tight. The gym people may try to convince you that's the best adjustment: nonsense! Turn the resistance down until you can pedal comfortably at your cruising speed.

Watch out for torn or lopsided seats; the latter can injure your hip and your knee because they change your position. People have actually been impaled or otherwise damaged on stationary bicycles when the seat cover parted company with the seat frame.

Seat height: many gym machines have seat posts that adjust by removing a steel pin and inserting it into holes placed about an inch apart.

If you have to choose between having the seat too high or too low, try the lower setting and slide back on the seat.

Check for bent pedals or cranks, which will cause the foot to change position with every revolution. This can be murder on the knees.

If the pedals have toestraps, use them if they allow the ball of the foot to be over the axle of the pedal. Check that the ball of the foot is behind the front of the knee when the pedal is in the three o'clock position.

Wear shoes: athlete's foot is a real danger when other people pedal barefoot. A quarter of the bones in the body are in the foot, so pedaling barefoot is the only thing worse than using running shoes. A stiff shoe, at least as stiff as a court sneaker, will distribute the strain of the pedal over a larger area.

If your shorts don't cover all of the seat, don't get on—rubbing against too large a seat can produce nasty rashes.

Avoid exercise class instructors who tell you that there is no gain without pain.

Another clue to watch out for is someone who takes the class proudly telling you that "I had pains in muscles that I didn't even know I had."

The best advice we can give you when you are told to "go for the burn," is to go take a shower instead of finishing the class.

EXERCISE BIKES VERSUS ERGOMETERS

Of the 2.5 million exercise bikes sold in 1985, less than 10% were quality, sturdily built machines, the kind that your orthopedist might recommend.

Since, as opposed to regular bicycles, there was no need to test them on the road, some manufacturers apparently felt free to design anything that could be easily built with the tools and parts at hand.

What this means to you is that you must try them out very carefully. Some are only good for long-legged people, some only for short-legged people. (As with regular bikes, it is leg length rather than height that determines basic fit.)

Some are really junk that will shake you to pieces. Some are much better than that and work pretty well but make you feel as if you were pedaling in mud.

What Dr. Kenneth Cooper said way back in the 1977 edition of *The Aerobic Way* is still very good advice: "Test out the seat and handlebar position for comfort before you buy, and look for a good chainguard so your clothing won't get caught." He especially stressed that being able to adjust the resistance easily was very important.

The Difference Between Exercise Bikes and Ergometers

The difference between an exercise bicycle and an ergometer is that on an exercise bicycle you have to guess at the tension, while an ergometer gives you that figure so you can repeat a workout and calculate the calories burned.

Ergometers are usually sturdier than exercise bikes, and they use metal flywheels which store energy better than the bicycle wheels on most exercise bikes.

The typical exercise bike creates resistance by having a bicycle brake grab the wheel or having a roller press against an inflated bicycle tire.

Ergometers create resistance either by using a disc brake or with a fabric band that is pulled against the outer surface of the wheel.

It is not the flywheel that makes a machine an ergometer. It is the calibration. Some of the more expensive exercise bikes use metal flywheels and some of the less expensive ergometers use Prony brakes instead of fabric bands. (Prony brakes are bicycle-type brakes that use large felt pads to press against the wheel.)

Ergometers have to be calibrated. The manufacturer had to calibrate it and may have to recalibrate it to keep it accurate.

If you're going to buy a $1000 machine, find out if they have a calibration kit or if the people

27

selling it are willing to recalibrate it. Get that in writing on your receipt.

Should You Get an Ergometer?

While an ergometer doesn't feel like riding a real bike, most of them have a nice cushy feel that tells you that you are working on a quality machine that helps you sustain a good pedaling rhythm.

But is it worth the additional expense—three, four, five times what a typical exercise bike costs?

For the very strong an ergometer offers more "training top" than an exercise bike. You can pedal at a higher resistance and at a higher pedaling rate than on an exercise bike with less precise parts.

The one thing the big expensive machines have going for them is tremendous sturdiness and solidity. And if you're not athletically inclined, or in a condition to even think about that sort of thing, as a therapeutic device they aren't that expensive.

If you're really involved with calorie counting, you may have to pay dearly for having this read out on a computer. On electronic machines you punch in your weight, so the readout is fairly accurate.

The added instrumentation of expensive ergometers seems like a poor investment if it's just more accurate calorie counting you want to do.

Heart-rate monitors and bicycle computers can give you the same information at much less cost. And they are getting better and cheaper very rapidly. Soon you will be able to buy ones that will print out very detailed information and will communicate with your personal computer.

If you are suffering from high blood pressure, heart disease, arthritis, back pain, obesity or a number of other medical problems, your doctor can prescribe an ergometer to use as part of a rehabilitation program and/or to fulfill an exercise prescription. Buying one then becomes a medical expense; you might be able to get it on Medicare or from your union or company health plan; in any case you should be able to deduct it from your income tax.

What they're all going to think about your getting a $2000 racing bike to go with your $75 wind-load simulator is another story.

A sturdy, well-built ergometer would be a nice thing to have, but unless it is necessary because of your health a well-built stationary bicycle that fits you is all that you need.

Living Without Calibration

On an exercise bike some tension is necessary for the pedaling to feel right, and a very small difference will feel too high or too low. With some practice this point will be easy to find.

Later, after you have learned to pedal faster,

you will be able to make very fast adjustments to higher tensions.

If the starting tension is so high that it stops you from picking up more pedal revolutions, it should be lowered; save the additional resistance for when you are stronger.

Do You Have to Buy New, Anyway?

Old bicycles get trashed, but old exercise cycles just get stored away. You can usually borrow one and may have trouble getting people to take it back!

The community center's spring cleaning sale will bring out some of these dinosaurs—some even pre-World War II. You would be amazed at the variety that were made. Don't turn up your nose at them, but be careful. Some may not have been used in the thirty-five years since Uncle Fred passed away yet really only need oiling and adjustment to be better than any of the cheap, flimsy modern ones.

Expensive Machines

Some of the expensive indoor bicycles use either a double flywheel and/or magnetic damping, cams or such to even out the result of uneven pedaling.

The idea is that by leveling and evening out the load the exercise becomes more aerobic and anerobic strength is not called upon. (This is why we stress the need for smooth, even pedaling throughout the book.)

Some manufacturers claim that because the exercise is more aerobic a shorter workout is possible and they offer various experimental proofs to back this up.

We think that it would probably be safe to ignore these claims, but if the machines do even out the tiny differences in pedal pressures and therefore call for less anerobic effort, you should be able to work out longer and reach your heart target rate sooner.

If one of these machines feels right to you, it might be easier to start and progress on it than on a more traditional ergometer or exercise bike. Since these machines are usually sold and rented through fitness centers it might make sense to rent one.

RUMMAGE-SALE BIKE. Fifty-year-old Rollfasts turn up frequently at rummage sales. With any old exercise bike, check that the wheel can be centered easily.

TO RENT OR TO BUY

The industry claims that three out of four people who rent end up buying. That can be an expensive way of buying something second hand. If you rent a machine, you may have to deal with a very persuasive salesperson later.

Renting a quality machine for a month or two and using it every other day should make you strong enough to go test other less expensive machines and to compare them with ergometers in the same price range. Perhaps by then a simpler and cheaper exercise bike or a bicycle with a wind-load simulator will fill your needs.

To avoid aches and pains and even permanent injury to knees, hands and back, it's very important to have a bike that can be adjusted to fit. No one model is right for everybody, not even through the entire range of adjustments.

If you're debating between two models, rent each for a month.

Renting shouldn't stop you from shopping around.

Alternatives to Renting

Most gyms, Ys, health clubs and spas let you have a fairly long trail visit. Take advantage of this to give the exercise bike(s) there as long a workout as your level of fitness can stand.

Have a full tryout at a friend's house. Or at several friends' houses, if they have different machines.

Buy an Exercise Bike at a Quality Bike Store

People who work in bike stores are used to people who are fussy about bike fit. They sell top-quality clothes and accessories as well. Then again, good equipment doesn't need as much fiddling with to work properly as cheap equipment, so bike stores will be reluctant to sell a real piece of trash, since they wouldn't want to fix it; department stores feel no such reluctance.

While you're there, ask to see a wind-load simulator and to ride a bike on it. Don't worry if your principal complaint is getting on or off the machine. When you're home, you can solve that problem by putting a little stool next to it. Ask if you can bring your bike in to try it again.

There are dozens of different brands of exercise bikes and ergometers, and no one knows how many different models, so it can be a help that a bike store usually has a smaller selection. If you don't see one you like, your friendly neighborhood bike store has people who can advise you on bike fit and what changes of seat, handlebar, etc., are possible or necessary for a quality machine you buy somewhere else. They may also warn you off certain mass market machines.

A bike store mechanic can probably get a

machine operating better than a salesperson in a department or sporting goods store. Before you buy one in a box you should find out how much assembly is necessary.

TRYING THEM OUT

Before You Get On Any Indoor Bike:

Don't buy or even borrow a machine without trying it. The tryout should be at least 10 minutes long if you are strong enough to manage it.

Grasp the seat with both hands and make sure it can't move and doesn't tilt—you could have a bad fall.

Adjust the seat to the right height. Then firmly tighten the seat-post bolt/clamp/lever.

Turn the resistance to 0.

If Trying Out a Used Machine

Grease or oil the chain (spray lubricants are fine). Bike stores have special chain cleaners and lubes. Oil the chain from the inside, the part that rubs against the works; rub in with a cloth. You should be able to feel the chain rollers move.

Check for bent teeth on the chain ring and that the chain ring accepts the chain evenly during a complete revolution.

Check for bent pedals.

Check that the wheel is running true in the frame and that it's tight.

Checking Out a Machine

Make sure it fits you (see "Sizing Them Up" on page 32).

Turn the tension adjustment to 0. Then slowly, by working one leg against the other, listen to the noises that the machine makes.

There are two kinds of noise; one directly relates to your pedaling.

When you're changing speed, if something sounds as if it's grinding, it is.

Warm up on any new machine very slowly; if something is out of true you'll be able to both hear it and feel it before it does you any harm.

When you get up to 60 or 70rpm, stop pedaling and see how long it takes the wheel to stop rolling. If it stops right away, that's bad, because it means you would have to pedal very evenly to keep the weight going.

Some machines are relatively quiet at low speed but become coffee grinders and lease breakers at higher speeds. Check to see whether high speed increases the vibration and the noise level and whether the action still feels smooth enough so that you'd want to repeat it often.

The tension adjustment should be easy to read and should work very, very easily so that you can more or less come back to the same resistance level, even if you're guessing at it. It's not important to know what the resistance is, but it *is* important to be able to get back to the same intensity.

Find out if you have to return the tension lever to 0 to prevent stretching the cable or adjustment.

Ergometers have to be calibrated. The manufacturer had to calibrate it and may have to recalibrate it to keep it accurate. If you're going to buy one, find out if you can get a calibration kit or if the people selling it are willing to recalibrate it.

The wheel should run true and not wobble. Look for a wheel-centering adjustment.

SIZING THEM UP

Leg length—inseam—rather than height determines basic fit—as it does for regular bikes. For a more complete explanation, read the "Bike Fit" chapter.

The mystery is solved! We now know why so many exercise bicycles are in closets and garages. Even though the cheapest bicycles come in at least three frame sizes, ergometers and exercise bicycles are one-size-fits-all.

Everybody can't fit on every bike. But you won't know you don't really fit on one until you get strong enough to stay on for 20 minutes—that's when all the pains begin. And by that time you've had it too long to return it.

Because of all the different designs and configurations, however, you should be able to choose one that does fit, once you know what to look for.

Don't buy a machine that doesn't fit or can't be made to fit. It will only get less comfortable as you use it.

You don't want any machine that forces your knee to be in front of the pedal axle when you are cycling. This makes your knee bend too much, which is bad for it.

When a seat is raised or lowered, it also moves backward and forward. How much depends on the angle of the seat post.

Many exercise bikes copy the design of old-fashioned bicycles, and when the seat is lowered it is still quite far back. The only way short people can get comfortable is to adjust the seat so that it is too far forward.

While some indoor cycles copy bikes and are traps for short people, others are made so upright that they present a similar hazard to people with long legs.

To make sure your knee is in the proper relation with the pedal, put the bike in front of a mirror so you have a side view or have a friend check your position.

Your seat should be high enough to extend your leg almost fully with the ball of your foot on

Indoor cycling machines vary tremendously in dimensions and frame angles. The most important thing is getting the seat at the right height and in the right position.

the pedal. It should be low enough so you can pedal backward without rocking your hips.

The main market for exercise bicycles used to be gyms and the industry was unprepared for the home gym market. What is a necessity in a gym —an easily adjustable and positively locking seat height—can become a terrible hindrance when you want to fit one person onto a bike.

Many exercise bikes come with seats that seem absurdly large; these are meant to feel like a chair. For the unathletic, and for the overweight patient suffering from hypertension or heart disease, they are reassuring.

Cycles displayed in stores often have the seat clamp put on backward (facing the front of the bike rather than the rear). It's hard to say if this will improve the matter or make it worse, since it moves the seat forward.

Real bicycle seats have a rail so the seat can be adjusted forward and backward, but many indoor cycles have no such adjustment at all, which makes it all the more necessary to check your knee position before trying it out.

Also check to see if the seat can be tilted up and down. Being able to change these angles can be very important to your comfort after 20 minutes in the saddle.

Make sure you can reach the handlebars without straining.

COMPONENTS OF MACHINES

Seats

You have a fifty-fifty chance of getting used to the seat that comes with almost any ergometer or exercise bicycle.

Seats on the dozens of machines we examined ran from adequate to ridiculous for anyone who is used to riding a bike.

Machines with bolted-on seats are made for very heavy people, so that if they sit far back the seat won't catapult them to the ground. The tilt can be adjusted a little bit by removing the bolts and adding or subtracting washers.

Comfort would be improved tremendously for many people by replacing the seat with a padded anatomical touring seat or by using that old standby, the Brooks B-72 that used to be standard equipment on good 3-speed bikes. Both types come in a men's and a women's model.

Spenco's saddle pad cushions well and dampens vibration. It is thick, so it adds to seat height. It comes in three widths to fit racing, touring and wide exercise seats.

Seat Posts

Drilled-out seat posts are a safety feature if you are very heavy (over 200 pounds). If you can't stay on the bike very long, exact seat-height fit doesn't matter that much, but if you are into serious training, we think these should be avoided.

If your bike has a seat post with inch-apart adjustments, platform pedals and/or a thinner seat would help in getting a better fit. Or, with a file or drill, you can expand the next higher hole into a slot to lower the seat.

Pedals

Replacing the pedals on most of the machines we examined would improve pedaling performance and efficiency. You remove pedals by turning the wrench clockwise. Take them with you to the bike store, as there are two "standard" threadings.

Either buy the grippy kind that are used on kids' BMX bikes or the rattrap styles that are used on 10-speeds. Racing pedals are 3 inches wide, touring pedals are 4 inches wide. Both take toeclips, which come in three sizes to fit different-size shoes.

Toeclips make it much easier to pedal hard and evenly, especially if the toestraps are snug. They let you know how you're doing and help you monitor the intensity and quality of a workout.

On some exercise bikes the pedals are much farther apart than on a bicycle, one reason the pedaling action feels different if you're used to riding a bike.

Handlebars

Make sure these adjust to fit you. Most of the machines available could use some padding. Foam rubber handlebar pads and padded bike gloves are sold at bicycle stores. Bike gloves leave your fingers free to turn pages or change channels.

Resistance Adjustment

Be sure you can reach and adjust this while pedaling. Both position and ease of adjustment vary a lot between models.

Flywheels

The larger and heavier the flywheel, the smoother and quieter the ride.

Heavier flywheels will work better and take longer to coast down than lighter ones, but the heavier and larger the flywheel the greater the need that the machine be level or placed on a level floor. The better machines have leveling screws and axle adjusters to make the wheel run straight.

35

OUR RECOMMENDATIONS

Our recommendation is to use what you have, can borrow or pick out at a yard sale. And that includes a 10-speed to team up with a wind-load simulator. (Since the bike never has to leave the house to work as an exercise machine, it doesn't have to be in great shape.)

But some people prefer the sturdiness a well-made stationary bicycle will give you; and they take up less room than a 10-speed and wind-load simulator.

Most people can probably get by with the stationary bicycle they already have, once they learn to use it in a sensible way.

It might take a while to dope out how to move the wheels so that the chain will run smoothly; it might just need some oiling, cleaning and running.

Using what you have will also help you make a wiser choice if you decide to get a new machine. And if you've really made the machine fit you, you may end up loving something you would have discarded.

Any money spent on pedals, toeclips or a new seat won't be wasted because the chances are that you'll need them on a new machine anyway.

Having two separate seats and seat posts makes sharing any bicycle exerciser simpler and is well worth the additional expense.

If you stood us against a wall and said that you'd shoot us unless we recommended a stationary bike, it would be one of these.

Exercise Bicycles with a 10-Speed Look

These machines were developed for the triathlete and bike-racer market. They have dropped handlebars, a racing seat and rattrap pedals with toeclips and toestraps.

They are moderately priced as ergometers go. Even though you might never want to ride a 10-speed, these machines still can represent your best buy because they use bike parts, so you can change the stem, seat and handlebars to give you correct fit.

You can have all the advantages of the adaptability of bike-store equipment without riding in the dropped position. In spite of what you see on TV commercials, 90% of bicycle riding is done on the top part of the bars.

If you want a more upright position, turn the handlebars up (or get new upright ones) and add a 10-speed touring seat.

The active person who is fairly fit and wants to do some serious training will probably like these bikes better than the regular wide-seat models.

They allow for all the adjustments possible on a regular 10-speed and take up a lot less room. They are quieter than wind-load simulators and vibrate very little, even at high-rev speeds and with heavy resistance.

The nicest feature is the big dial that lets you constantly monitor your pedal revolutions. The best and safest way to become fit on an indoor bicycle is to get pedal speed up to at least 80-85.

They allow you to repeat a workout and monitor your training program. The rev counters go up higher than those for regular ergometers because they're designed for the triathlete. This is a useful feature for everyone since it encourages you to increase your intensity by increasing pedal rate rather than by increasing resistance.

The difference between the cheaper and the more expensive models seems to be the added flywheel weight, disc-brake resistance as opposed to strap-generated resistance, and a calorie counter.

At last! Ergometers built like 10-speed bikes and built by top names in the ergometer field! While we didn't get to ride all the brands, our personal favorite was the Tunturi Executive Sport Model Racing Ergometer.

The Schwinn Excelsior XR-7

It's well built, works well and sells for under $300.

It's as much exercise bike as you'll ever need.

It weighs 55 pounds and has a very stable base with leveling adjustments, a good feature that is missing on many machines that cost a lot more.

It has a heavy metal flywheel and an easy-to-reach, easy-to-use resistance adjuster.

The handlebar can be raised and lowered and tilted forward and back.

Older models came with calibrated seat posts and a lever lock. The later models have the inch-apart adjustments adopted by many of the name manufacturers.

Because the XR-7 is sold and guaranteed by the Schwinn network of trained bicycle dealers and mechanics, you can expect expert help with fit and changing the pedals and the seat, which may be comfortable but is on the largish side.

BCA, the Bicycle Corporation of America, offers the Slimline 5, a similar machine that might be worth looking at. Also similar is the Panasonic EX-1000.

USE YOUR OWN 10-SPEED

You don't have to be able to ride a bike to use a bike on a wind-load simulator. An open frame—woman's or mixte (unisex)—would be a good choice because getting on and off is easier.

Just because you don't ride a bike is no reason to miss out on this inexpensive exercise machine.

It is much easier to wheel a bicycle to the bike store for adjustments or repair than wait for the repairman to come service your 100-pound ergometer.

A bicycle with a wind-load simulator would be a framework for the new electronics, such as bicycle calculators and heart-rate monitors, intended for bicycle use. It would allow you to benefit from the wide choice of improved seats, handlebars, padding and other products made for the enormous leisure bicycling industry.

Almost as soon as there were bicycles, people wanted training stands so they could be used for indoor exercise.

By the 1890s, when the bicycle was "King of the Road," home trainers and rollers looked and worked pretty much like the ones on sale today.

Rollers

Rollers, which are a sort of portable indoor road, have three rollers connected by a belt on which you ride the bicycle.

Home Trainers

Home trainers—there are two sorts—both use the back wheel to drive a resistance element. The simpler type, still sold in discount stores and by mail order, lifts the back wheel onto a framework that supports the bicycle; the bicycle rides on a small spring-loaded roller that is very hard on the tire and on you, because it produces a very bouncy ride.

Don't go out and buy one of these. But if you have one it is useful until you get a wind-load simulator. If you have one, put on the fattest tire you can get to cushion the shock.

The elegant European home trainers—some cost hundreds of dollars—use much larger rollers. The two-roller models are the best.

Wind-Load Simulators

There's been a revolution in indoor bicycle training in the past few years. Racer-Mate had a marvelously simple idea: the wind-load trainer.

With the bicycle on a stand, use the back wheel to turn a ventilator cage with blades to catch the air. The faster the back wheel moves the more the air resistance builds up—exactly like biking outdoors.

Much lower cost gets you something few ergometers or exercise bikes can give you:

A machine you can update as new electronic equipment comes out, and easily interchangeable bicycle parts to make the bike a perfect fit.

In order to perfect your position on the bike you'll be able to try out and adjust equipment—stems, seat height, cleat angle —where the tools are.

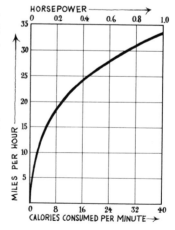

WIND-LOAD SIMULATORS

If you can't get comfortable on any of the available ergometers, you should get a bike and a wind-load simulator. This setup can offer you tremendous choice in the way of equipment. You now have something you can tailor to your body. When next year's more comfortable saddle comes out, just get it and put it on the bike.

On most exercise bicycles, riding feels like riding a bike with the brake stuck, and the more resistance you work with the less it feels like riding a real bicycle. On a wind-load simulator, the resistance increases with the gearing, which makes it feel like riding a real bike.

You may not realize it, but on a bicycle you are pedaling through a sea of air. Air resistance increases rapidly. At 15 miles an hour half of your energy is used to overcome air resistance. At 18mph it increases to 80%. At 20mph wind resistance is almost 90%.

Wind-load simulators make the effort of pedaling indoors match the effort of pedaling a bicycle on the road. If you can do a 40-second sprint in a high gear outside, that's what you'll be able to do with the wind-load simulator. If 20 minutes of almost hard pedaling at 75% of your target rate is what you can do on the road, that's about what you'll be able to do with a wind-load simulator. So it's easy to figure out how you're doing. Even the casual cyclists can draw on their experience and memory to know what's an extremely hard effort to avoid. But check your pulse anyway!

On a wind-load simulator the back tire makes contact with a shaft that turns a squirrel cage. The faster it turns the greater the air resistance: that's the wind load. Unless you're superstrong it simulates the resistance between 12mph and 25mph quite well.

The first version of the Racer-Mate attaches the squirrel cage to the seat post of the bicycle and can be used either as a stationary bicycle on a stand or as resistance for a bicycle on rollers.

Turbo-Trainer placed the squirrel cage roller on a stand, which made it easier to change bicycles. This is a useful selling device for bike stores, which can let you try out different machines.

Wind-load simulator rollers and home trainers are already on the market. Can wind-load exercise bicycles be far behind? They'll probably be on the market in 1988-89.

There are wind-load trainers that will take mountain bikes and at least one that a 20-inch BMX bike will fit on.

Most bicycle computers have rear-mounting kits so they can be used with wind-load simulator training stands.

As of late 1986 there were at least ten versions of

WIND-LOAD SIMULATOR.
The original Racer-Mate—insert shows how the
"squirrel cage" is pulled against the rear wheel.
Many people still consider this the best design.
It can be used with rollers. For higher resistance
it can be combined with a wind-load simulator
where the squirrel cage is under the wheel.

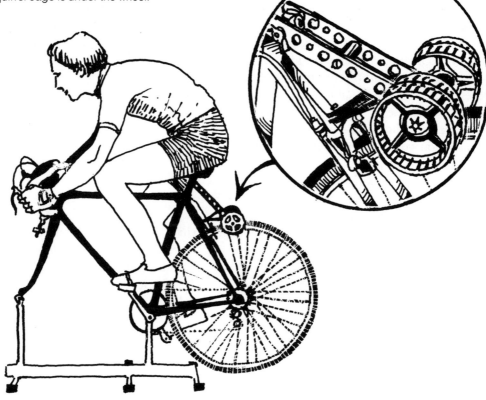

wind-load simulating devices. Every bike doesn't fit every version. If the cables are routed underneath, or if a bottom bracket has been lightened, as it is in many racing bikes, the support might not attach properly.

One way around this is to raise the rear wheel and attach the bike to a stand that grasps the down tube. Since the bike rests on its front wheel and can still be steered, such stands have very wide bases.

With better bikes that have Allen-key-adjusting seat posts and handlebars, it takes only a couple of minutes to adjust away the downhill effect.

Mountain bikes, 3-speeds and 10-speeds that use 26-inch wheels will all go slightly uphill on wind-load simulators built for 27-inch wheels.

A bike placed on the squirrel cage can skid at high speeds, resulting in loss of resistance. Therefore many bikers still prefer the original top-mounted Racer-Mate. To get even greater resistance, use it together with a bottom-mounted wind-load simulator. (Racer-Mate also makes a bottom-mounted one, the Racer-Mate II.)

There are several microroller trainers, on which the back wheel rides on two squirrel cage axles to create a very high resistance (or only on one for normal resistance).

As you get stronger, you may find that the 14-28 cluster is too widely spaced. If you need that cluster to ride the bike in the street, you may need another rear wheel...but you may have gotten so strong that a 14-23 will do.

The lighter wheel and just the right gears will be what's needed to pick up another five to ten more revs, because speeding up pedal revolutions is always the best way to increase work load on a stationary bicycle.

If you install a bicycle permanently on a wind-load simulator, you can do things to it to get comfortable that would make it very unsafe on the road. The bike doesn't need brakes or brake handles, and you can raise the stem above the safety point (1 1/2 inches inside).

If you try to use a bike that's way too small, you

PLATFORM FOR WIND-LOAD SIMULATOR.
Here the wind-load simulator is mounted on plywood for increased stability.

43

might have to screw the whole stand down onto something or it could tip over backward when you sit up straight on it.

There's no need to be afraid of falling with toe-clips, or to worry about how to get out of them as you might in traffic.

Your first bike is nearly always a mistake that gives you a better idea about what you really want. It's okay to use it as a trainer as long as the mistake wasn't getting a frame that's way too big or too small because there is a much wider range of adaptability on a wind-load simulator than there is on the road. A seat all the way down to the top tube is dangerous on the road but only inconvenient in the house. If you have too much of a reach for the handlebars, you can bring them around to face you or change the stem.

For under $200 you can put together an indoor bicycle setup that's better than anything you can buy for much more. A yard-sale 10-speed or the one that you would have sold if you had a yard sale will do nicely. No brakes and no front wheel are needed as long as the frame and the pedal cranks are straight and the back wheel is true. Don't give up on cranky derailleurs that didn't work well on the road; once on the wind-load simulator stand, they may work all right.

Check out the ads in the bicycling magazines for the latest developments and check their mail-order ads for bargains. But don't blame your dealer if he can't get a specific model. Ads are often published before the item is in the hands of the distributors. Sometimes a late-breaking technical problem may hold up shipping for months.

As you get healthier from doing aerobic endurance exercise on an indoor bike you feel better about yourself. About this time you start thinking you deserve a present. We can't think of a nicer present than a new bicycle.

ROLLERS

Suppleness, extremely high leg speed, the automatic censoring of poor form and pedaling are some reasons rollers turn you into a better runner or bike rider.

Until the invention of the wind-load trainers in the late seventies, bicycle enthusiasts did indoor winter training on rollers, the only alternative to bicycle exercisers. They were (and are) popular because they let you check bike fit and position indoors where the tools are, as well as practicing bike-handling skills.

With practice you can learn to ride no hands, signal, look behind you and drink from your water bottle while pedaling. The show-stopping trick is to be able to change your shirt.

Rollers consist of a frame with three rollers that

the bicycle rides on; a huge rubber band or belt connects the middle back roller to the front one; when the bike is ridden this drives the front wheel, making balancing possible.

Rollers are tricky to learn to use and easy to fall off of at first.

Despite tall tales to the contrary, the bike doesn't roll off them and dart across the room.

Rollers are cheap, under $100 and up.

The terrible noise they used to make has been cured in the modern ones by the use of sealed bearings.

Steps, bike holders, blowers and wind-resistant attachments are available.

Learning to Ride

Riding rollers is a bit like bicycling on ice. A little mistake in balance must be corrected by a little countermove; too big an adjustment and off you come. It's not as dangerous as it sounds. It's

THE CYCLODROME.
The hit of the 1893 Columbia Exhibition in Chicago. The large roller made the bicycles easy to ride. Note the miniature cyclodrome that reflects the positions of the men riding bicycles on the rollers.

annoying and damages your bike-handling pride.

Most people can learn after a few sessions. Either have someone hold you up or practice in a narrow hall or doorway or next to a counter or bar you can lean on. Having a helper is easier than the hallway method, because it is difficult to let go of the wall and keep your balance.

Everything happens very fast on the rollers. For that reason, high gears are used—gears that are 10% to 20% higher than what you might use on the road. And because there is very litle resistance, pedal revs can reach from 100 to over 160. With practice, you can use normal gears and normal pedaling rates.

If your pedaling form or your position on the bike isn't good, you'll bounce on the seat and have to make constant steering adjustments to stay on.

Important Improvements

Like everything else in biking, rollers have undergone a revolution in the last ten years. They're quieter and smoother.

The resistance cage from the original version of the Racer-Mate, the invention that created the wind-load trainer industry, attaches to the seat post, so that it can be used on a roller, and adds the resistance necessary to be able to stay up at lower revs and lower gears. To the suppleness and speed training the traditional roller work pro-duced was added power.

Several new types of rollers have wind-speed resistance cages directly attached or driven by the rollers.

The frightening thing about rollers is that you're so far from the ground. The added six inches seems like much more, and the need for quick little movements adds to the unnatural feeling. The steps that fit some rollers make getting on and off easier, but it was the home gym movement that provided the idea that makes rollers available to almost anyone who can balance on a bike.

Some bright designer thought of building the rollers into the floor or into a platform. By decreasing the distance that it is possible to fall, it is easier to learn even without the added resistance of the Racer-Mate.

At a recent trade show we saw several people just get on and ride a bike with the rollers built into a platform. Some had never been on rollers but were still able to ride for a minute or two

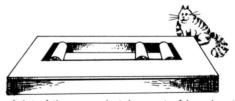

A lot of the scare is taken out of learning to use rollers by building a plywood platform for them to fit into. Some rollers come with accessory steps.

before they made a mistake that took them off.

A Sweaty Business

You sweat like a pig. Perhaps more than in any other form of indoor cycling. A puddle collects on the floor under your chin. Not that this is bad.

Because you sweat so heavily, it's a good idea to tape a washcloth over the bicycle's headset; sweat can actually weld the stem so tight that it is impossible to move. Sweatbands, a towel around your neck, bike gloves with knitted backs all allow you to mop up.

Setting Up Your Bike

A close match between the rollers and where the tires set is necessary. Rollers usually have some front-end adjustment, but it may be necessary to change to a fatter or a thinner tire to make the perfect match.

A lightweight tire and rim are preferable to keep revolving weight down and extreme high revs possible. Conversely, it may be easier to learn with heavy tires.

Important Note:

When you buy a set of rollers, get an extra belt. They're not always interchangeable between brands. The bicycle industry is a collection of small firms that sometimes just disappear, leaving customers in search of spare parts up the creek.

HOME TRAINERS

There are many versions of this European machine, some very nicely made and really nifty-looking. On most, the front wheel is removed; the bicycle is supported and rolls on one or two small rollers; resistance is produced by braking the rollers or by a sprung roller pressing against the tire.

Never really successful in the United States

TRICYCLE HOME TRAINER. 1876 home trainer for an iron-tired tricycle. Resistance was produced by pressure from a brake shoe against the rear roller. *From authors' archive file.*

market, there are probably several warehouses full of them, and the fitness boom will bring them back on the market as the latest thing.

If you don't weigh very much (under 150) and pedal smoothly, you can get a comfortable workout on one of these. The pounding can be reduced by putting a fatter tire on the back wheel or by using one of the new padded anatomical seats. Padding the handlebars with foam tape or putting foam grips on them reduces some of the pressure on your hands.

The action on the better version of these machines is quite smooth, but the result is still a very hard ride. Using pedals with toeclips makes your connection with the machine better and helps damp out some of the vibration.

Some home trainers leave on the front wheel. Since the back wheel has to be raised, you are pedaling downhill, which may take some getting used to, besides putting more weight on your hands.

Try to put a big book under the front wheel to counteract some of the downhill effect. If you let a little of the air out of your front tire, the front wheel will stay in one place.

If that doesn't help enough, tilt the seat and the bars to bring everything back parallel to the ground. But now your bike's no longer set up to ride outside. Allen key microadjusting seat post and stem make changing back fairly simple.

THE FUTURE IS NOW

Now for something completely different.

Bicycling has always been a game that attracted the basement inventors. It is a business with many small manufacturers, where even the larger ones make a surprising number of products.

A bicycle manufacturer may build or put together dozens of different models and may buy parts from dozens of sources.

Bicycling is also a lifelong passion; it has its own little world, one that loves to talk endlessly about bicycles and bits of bicycles.

A bicycle seems so simple that there doesn't seem to be any reason why it shouldn't work perfectly.

If only...

So every idea has been tried before and gets constantly reinvented.

But the chances of success of a "new" idea or product are slim. Just as in any other business or racket, luck and good timing plus good business skills are needed.

With the interest in fitness and the new bicycle boom, the chances of a new idea catching on have greatly increased.

The Road Machine

Racer-Mate revolutionized indoor bicycling with its introduction of the wind-load simulator. The product was so simple that a whole little industry has started, with at least a dozen wind-load simulators now on the market.

Larry Brown, the developer of the Power-Cam bicycle transmission, took the idea of the wind-load simulator in a different direction. Why not build a stand for a windload simulator that supports a 10-speed the way the back wheel does and takes the place of a wheel?

The Road Machine has a startlingly simple

THE ROAD MACHINE.
A wind-load simulator with a balanced flywheel mechanism that completely replaces the back wheel of a 10-speed bike.

design. It fits into the dropouts that hold the back wheel in place. It has a built-in rear gear cluster that drives the built-in wind-load simulator.

This solves the problem of mounting bikes of different sizes to a wind-load simulator or damaging the bike with the supports of the stand.

The Road Machine, because it is a stand-alone wind-load simulator, can drive other types of fitness machines. Houdille, the manufacturer of the Road Machine, also builds a stationary bicycle and a rowing machine that the Road Machine fits. Serious rowers already know about wind-resistance machines—The Concept II is a wind-load simulator and has many avid fans.

Recumbent Stationary Bicycles

Recumbent bicycles have been around since the 1900s and are still used in the International Human Powered Speed Championships. There are several modern versions on the market.

On a recumbent you pedal sitting down with your legs in front of you rather than underneath you. There is a backrest to push against.

What you have is an exercise machine in which you can sit the way you sit in a chair. Pushing against the backrest lets you pedal harder.

Since finding a seat that is comfortable is one of the most difficult things to do when you're riding any kind of bicycle, the recumbent might win a lot of fans.

AMF's Benchmark 940 Cycle is an example of a recumbent bicycle ergometer. Designed by an industrial designer, the Benchmark 940 has many advanced features. Resistance is created by electric damping. The "flywheel" is just there as an indicator that the machine is working and for sound effects.

Because the electromagnetic resistance replaces rollers and belts and chains, the machine is very quiet.

Because the seat pushes straight back, the Benchmark 940 can be used by short people and people as tall as six feet seven.

The backrest makes it usable by those with back problems who could not possibly use a standard type of bicycle exercise machine, assuming it can be put on a platform so that they don't have to get on the floor to get on and off it.

The manufacturer claims that there are many advantages to having the legs at the level of the heart. One advantage mentioned is that on a regular bicycle the maximum force that can be applied to the pedal is the weight of the body, while on a recumbent the limit is the strength of the legs.

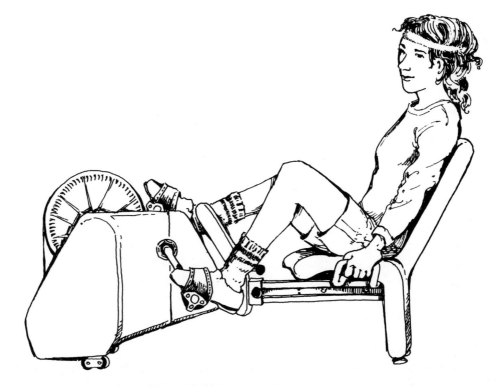

FIRST OF THE NEW RECUMBENTS.
The AMF Benchmark 940 cycle fits people from
4′10″ to 6′7″ and features an electronic readout
of miles per hour, calories consumed, etc.

BEFORE YOU START

BASICS OF TRAINING

Aerobic training/cardiovascular exercise does all the good things that the doctors and all those runners claim it does.

In six to eight weeks, with as few as three 30-minute workouts a week, you can start to turn your health around as you experience the training effect and build endurance.

There are three basic ways to build endurance: how long, how hard and how often you exercise. Technically, they are referred to as duration, intensity and frequency. A change in any one of them causes a change in the others. If, for example, you roll along at a faster clip than usual, you shouldn't do it for as long a time.

People seldom get hurt by gradually increasing the amount of time they spend on the machine; on the other hand, they can easily get hurt by increasing the intensity of a workout. How frequently you work out also makes a difference: alternating a hard and an easy day is often necessary to give joints and muscles time to recover.

Building endurance means increasing the ability of the muscles to use oxygen (aerobic means "with air") and using the energy stored in the body for longer times and at increasing intensity.

Runners use the sweat and talk test.

You've gone aerobic when you start to break into a sweat; and to ensure that you don't overdo it, you should have enough breath left over to talk. The talk test is a guarantee that you really aren't overdoing it and still have control of your breathing.

When the breathing becomes too rapid for talking you are leaving the aerobic area for the anerobic (no air); this is your body's involuntary reaction to overdoing speed or intensity of effort. You're going into oxygen debt and are tapping your limited supply of anerobic energy—the energy that's stored in your muscles for a rapid sprint. In an all-out workout, this energy is burned off slowly; since it takes about forty-eight hours to replace itself, it is the basis for the hard-easy day training theory.

On an indoor bike you have a simple method of checking your workouts. You can take your pulse while you are doing it.

To get a training effect, your heart must be beating at at least 60% of its maximum, figured by subtracting your age from 220 and multiplying the result by 0.6.

After a while, when you begin to feel the training effect, the number of revolutions necessary to produce this talk-test rate will increase as the number of breaths decreases. Test for this: take your pulse to make sure that you have not exceeded the 85% heart rate.

Trying to get a good workout by thrashing around at a high resistance before you have solved the problems of being comfortable and staying on the bike is the surest way to discourage yourself and makes it difficult to continue a reasonable training schedule.

Ignore those dials, they're just a temptation to overdo, although the speedometer is useful, not to know that you're doing 23mph (you're not really going 23mph anyway), but to know that you're pedaling at a steady rate. If the speed fluctuates wildly, your pedaling rate is uneven.

Besides, the measurements that indicators on stationary bicycles show have nothing to do with you. What's important is what *you* are doing: your heartbeat, how many revs you are producing, your breathing (can you pass the talk test?); these are more important than what some dial tells you is your mileage.

Man is unique among the running animals in that his breathing is independent of his running gait. Man's erect position frees him from the one-for-one breathing rate of the horse or the dog.

A certain pedaling or running rate will feel right because the breathing and the gait have found a tempo that is natural and easy.

A bike, if you sit on it correctly, supports more than half your weight. This frees the large muscles in your legs, which help hold you up, to spin your legs. This is also why it is so easy to overdo on a bike; you are freed from gravity.

And that's why indoor biking is so good for circulation, the heart, the whole body. It lowers blood pressure and helps you lose weight. And it does all this without stressing your joints the way jogging does.

Endurance/aerobic training shows how our bodies deal positively with stress—by getting stronger. Once you gain endurance you face life with joy and energy, and the negative effects of other types of stress, from chronic fatigue to high blood pressure, lessen their hold on your body.

F-I-T: Frequency, Intensity and Time are all interrelated in training. Try to increase only one of these measures at a time.

Frequency—how often you do a workout. As you get fit this should be increased from every other day to alternating hard and easy days. Six days are sufficient!

Intensity—how hard you work. Pedal rpms (speed) and resistance or gearing are measures of intensity and should be gradually increased. It is better for the knees to work on getting pedal revolutions up to 80 before you increase intensity. (Increasing speed is better for the knees than increasing resistance.)

Time—how long you work each time. The duration (that's where endurance comes from) should also be increased gradually to avoid overtraining symptoms.

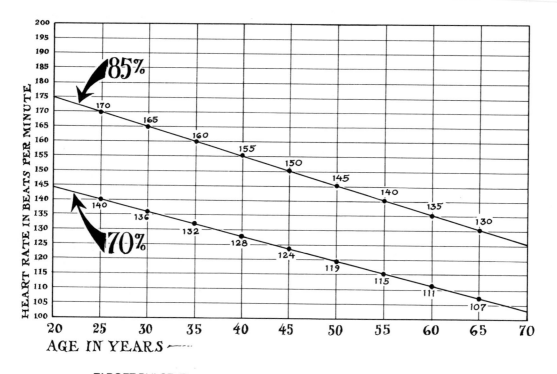

TARGET PULSE. The aerobic training zone is between 60 percent and 85 percent of your maximum heart rate. This is figured by subtracting your age from 220, then multiplying by the percentage wanted. Find the numbers for your age; then see how many beats that is for each ten seconds. The nearer your resting pulse is to your aerobic zone, the worse shape you are in, and the more careful you have to be.

HOW TO TAKE YOUR PULSE

The most important reason to take your pulse is to check that you're not approaching, much less exceeding, your age-determined maximum heart rate (220 minus your age times 85%)

Find the correct figures for your heart rate at 60%, 75% and 85%. Write them down on a piece of tape and tape them onto your exercise bike where you can see them as you are pedaling.

Part of your training will be to find out how you feel at each of these rates. At what percentage do you start to sweat? To open your mouth to breathe? To feel breathless? Once you know how you feel when you enter the aerobic zone and when you are approaching the outer limits of safety, you will not have to take your pulse often.

As you get more and more fit, you will find that it takes more effort both to get to the aerobic level and to get to the danger zone. That shows you have greater endurance, and *that's* what the training effect is all about.

It's all right to stop pedaling to take your pulse; just get ready to take it before you stop. As soon as you have checked it, start pedaling slowly again. Take fifteen or thirty seconds to get back to that comfortable but hard-rolling speed you had just before you stopped.

Take the pulse on the radial artery of the wrist that runs below the thumb. (Some people can see it pulsating if they bend their hand slightly.) Place your watch so that the face is on the inside of the wrist. Rest your wrist in the palm of your other hand. Your three fingers should be able to find your pulse easily. Be sure to use the fingers, not the other thumb. Take two fingers and press the wrist directly under the joint of the thumb.

It may be easier to find the carotid pulse in the neck, by the outside of the Adam's apple, but easy does it. Pressing hard on the carotid artery can cause the blackout beloved by mystery story writers. The heart slows by reflex, dropping the blood pressure, causing the blackout.

It is sometimes possible to see the pulse in the forehead; light pressure on this spot can sometimes detect the resting pulse.

Count the pulsations for 15 seconds and multiply by 4 (or 10 seconds and multiply by 6). It helps to have a watch or clock with a sweep second hand. For a rough count, count for 6 seconds and add 0; counting for 12 seconds and dividing by 2 gives a more accurate count. Bear in mind that the heart slows rapidly and that only the first 10 to 15 seconds equal the final seconds of effort.

Soon you will be able to gauge by your breathing, sweating and pedaling whether you're at your training rate. Then you need to check it only periodically.

THE RESTING PULSE –A MEASURE OF FITNESS

"The resting pulse can be considered a sign of general endurance; the lower it is, the better the endurance. An increase of 6 to 8 pulsations a minute indicates excess fatigue or the beginning of overtraining or illness.

"In a healthy adult, the pulse rate is 60 to 80 a minute; in a trained athlete, 40 to 60; it is more rapid in the evening than in the morning. Physical effort, meals, fear and other emotions speed it up. During illness the pulse generally accelerates," according to Jean-Pierre de Mondenard, M.D., author, columnist, medical answer man of French cycling.

"Every morning, before getting out of bed, count your pulse for 15 seconds. Wait 60 seconds, then stand up. Count it again for 15 seconds. Do this daily and record the difference between the lying-down pulse and the standing-up pulse. If there is a sudden rise in the difference between them, it is a sign that your body has not recovered from yesterday's training," says Edmund R. Burke, Ph. D., director of the Center for Science, Medicine and Technology of the United States Cycling Federation.

If you are on a schedule that alternates hard and easy days, check your resting pulse on the morning of the hard day to see if you've recovered from the last hard day's workout.

HEART-RATE MONITORS

Heart-rate monitors and electronically operated speedometers come built in on expensive machines and are also available as add-ons for bicycles.

Don't Buy One that You Can't Take Back

Don't buy anything that you can't test thoroughly and return. (Although it might be difficult to return a sweat-soaked EKG detector that straps around your chest.)

Except for some wristwatch monitors, units have two parts—the detector that reads the signal and the monitor that is usually mounted on the handlebars.

At the end of a workout it's very easy to forget to take off your heart-rate monitor. The wires pull off easily and can get caught in the works of the bicycle. For this reason we recommend that you get a unit with a detector that isn't directly wired but plugs into the reading unit or, state of the art and still expensive, a wireless model that works by remote control.

Beware of inexpensive mail-order pulse detectors ($20 and under). They seldom are accurate . . . even when they work.

Wristwatch Monitors

Wristwatch heart monitors are about the least expensive type available. They can give you useful information if you don't take them too much at their word and trust their readings completely. And you don't have to worry about wires when you get off the bike.

Like all pulse-type meters, they are light sensitive, so changing light will influence the reading.

They may not take kindly to vibration, so if you want to read them during your workout you may have to stop pedaling.

All in all, they are fairly accurate from the resting zone to about 125-140, but they may be so affected by the vibration of an indoor bicycle that only the lower readings can be trusted, which may not warn you that you are entering the danger zone.

Your pulse is always there to check out how the reading of a heart-rate monitor compares to your actual pulse.

Finger or Ear Pulse Detectors

Thimble or clamp monitors read the pulse in your finger and ones that clip onto your earlobe are more accurate than wristwatch detectors but share their weaknesses. Some emit warning zone signals between 150 and 200.

Rub your finger or ear to get the blood going before you take a reading; sweat or numbness can influence readings.

The ones that have been around awhile use a lot of batteries and use them up fast. Newer models have improved electronics so you're not often faced with a dead battery or a weak signal.

Heart monitors for runners ought to be able to stand up to the vibration of indoor bicycles.

EKG Chest-Wrap Detectors

EKG chest-wrap detectors pick up the electrical signal that fires the heart and makes it beat. The strap holding the detector must be worn firmly around the chest.

These are more accurate than pulse detectors and give better readings at higher heartbeat rates. It does take a little time to get used to wearing them.

Some high-tech models send the heart reading by radio to a wristwatch that works like a stopwatch. Readings and time done are stored and can be called up like the times on any electronic stopwatch.

Some machines pick up what they read as an irregularity—and flash 0 . . . no pulse!

Bicycle Computers

High-tech in the bicycling world are bicycle computers ($30 to $100) with accessory heart-rate monitors. Both pulse type and EKG are available. The detectors plug into the computer. Total cost, $150 to $300 (far less than what you would pay toward an ergometer with this feature.)

Bicycle computers are at least as accurate as the speedometer in your car. They are much more accurate than the wire- or cable-driven ones used on exercise bikes and on some ergometers.

Bicycle computers use magnets attached to the wheel to read miles per hour and distance traveled or to the chain wheel to read pedal revolutions. Some adjust to different-size wheels so you may be able to attach one to your stationary bike.

Simple ones combine a speedometer and an odometer that can be reset. Expensive ones average speed, read pedal revolutions and have some stopwatch functions.

If you are using a wind-load simulator, you will have to buy a rear-mounting accessory to fit the detector to your bicycle. They are sold for most models.

Meters with Calories-Consumed Readouts

The only way to really measure the calories consumed is by monitoring oxygen turnover, as is done in basal metabolism tests.

What the meters are showing is really the average calorie consumption for that heartbeat rate or for the energy consumed to do a certain amount of work if you weigh a certain amount.

In other words, the reading on meters with calorie consumption is an average for everyone who weighs the same amount and produces that particular amount of work.

In Development Now

The next generation of heart-rate detectors is still in the experimental stage. It will include direct-reading pulse counters with pressure-sensitive detectors that can be worn as wristbands or headbands. Only time can tell whether they can be made rugged enough to be used as exercise heart-rate monitors.

Bicyclists like gadgets and the market is large enough so that cheaper, better and more elaborate ones will be available.

TECHNIQUE

DANGER! BIKE IN THE HOUSE

While you are riding, keep all small children and pets in another room. Many a cat has been brained by a pedal when sneaking up behind someone. Children have gotten fingers caught in wheels. Dogs have been known to think it funny to nip at a flapping sweat-suit leg. Be especially careful with machines that drive a rear wheel, like rollers and wind-load machines.

Stationary bicycles are not designed to be kidproof. Don't ever let a child play with them; they are not toys. And don't leave a child unsupervised in the same room with one. A bike is a great temptation because of the moving parts and because turning the pedals makes the wheel move. Toddlers can pull the machine over on themselves if they pull on it to get to a standing position.

Bikes are among the most tripped over objects in a house, so keep them out of normal traffic areas. According to an old report from the Consumer Product Safety Commission, bicycles are the largest single cause of household accidents, worse than the kitchen ladder, cellar stairs and slippery bathtubs combined!

When Exercising on an Indoor Bike

Don't wear anything that hangs down where it can get caught in a wheel or pedal.

Tuck pants legs into socks.

Tie shoelaces to the side away from the pedal; knot the bow so it won't come undone.

Don't forget that you're strapped on when you go to answer the phone. If you're wearing either a heart monitor or earphones, remember to disconnect as you get off.

PEDALING

Forget all that stuff about how once you learn to ride a bike you never forget—it just doesn't apply to stationary cycling. No balancing tricks, no having to put your foot down on the ground, no worrying about how you're going to get your foot out of the toestrap; all you're left with on a stationary bike is how you sit on the seat and how you turn the pedals.

You're looking for a rate and a resistance that feel right for you. When you're pedaling smoothly and evenly, it's as if there were an egg on the pedal, and if you pedal smoothly you won't break it and it won't roll off.

When you're starting, you're limited by your fast walking speed. In fact most people can't even go as fast as that. That's where the temptation to push big gears or use greater resistance comes from: on a bicycle, trying to go fast; on an indoor bike, feeling you're getting a good workout.

Pedaling fast for a long time maximizes blood circulation.

The idea is to make perfect round circles with your legs.

Most people have gotten the idea someplace that riding a bike is a form of kicking: push, rest, push. On a hill this may be necessary, but on an indoor bike it is only useful during a stress test.

Push quite hard against the driving pedal, but try to avoid stamping, which stretches the muscles very rapidly and jiggles the upper body.

What you want to do is to pedal smoothly and not have to whip the foot around from one position to another during the pedal stroke.

Although we don't want you to stamp your feet when you pedal, you do have to exert enough pressure to move the pedal around. This means that even the soft rubber pedals that come with most indoor cycles will not protect bare feet or ones in soft running shoes.

Pedal with the ball of the foot, not with the toes or arch of the feet! The ball of the foot should be more or less over the axle of the pedal.

Like some skiers and runners, some bike racers make up for not having the agility to put out a lot of revs by muscling the bike around. This can make them burn out early. Smooth styles pay off in longevity in this sport. It takes practice, sometimes long practice, to get past the novice's 60 or so rpm. Pedal masters can go astonishingly fast—120 revs a minute.

Good pedaling is sort of like paddling along; pressure is gently applied on the drive part and released on the back stroke.

Ankling

You may have heard about ankling. Some bike riders make a whole big thing about it. The best thing to do is just forget it. If your seat is in the right place and your legs have good extension (80% straightened at the bottom of the rotation), you can't help but ankle.

Keep your foot level with the heel parallel to the ground as much as possible. Besides being more efficient, it is less likely to cause injury.

Toeclips

Toeclips are not just for the expert, toeclips helped make them expert!

STARTING OUT

Set up your bike properly.

Drink a glass of water before starting to avoid dehydration.

Use firm rubber-soled shoes that stick to the pedals.

If the saddle makes your bottom hurt the second or third time on it, bear with it before changing or adjusting your seat.

Have a clock in sight, preferably with a sweep second hand.

A *full-length mirror* or light set so you can watch your shadow on the wall is a good way to become a better pedaler and is actually an easier way to count your revs.

Have your TV set on or your reading rack filled; you should not get off until you have finished your planned time, as it is hard to get warmed up again.

Decide how fit you are. While cycling is useful to everyone, not everyone can start on the same level.

What level you start at depends on how fit you are. People who jog or play tennis regularly have much more endurance than people who have just been told by their doctor that they'd better do some exercise to get their blood pressure down.

You should be able to cycle for the same length of time you can run or swim. If you can jog for 30 minutes, you can cycle for at least 30 minutes. But since cycling uses muscles a bit differently, at the beginning we recommend doing the same length as your normal jog; only instead of stretching for 5 minutes, pedal at a slow speed to warm up, and again at the end to cool down. If this still produces leg pain, you're going at it too hard; you'll have to be a bit patient while you build up the cycling muscles.

Other sports are not as clearly connected to endurance. A half hour on a basketball or tennis court can be a real workout, but it's a lot of starting and stopping, most of it at sprinting speed. This doesn't necessarily build your endurance, but you should still be able to manage 15 minutes of indoor biking the first time out. (It will do wonders for your wind, by the way, once you're up to 40 minutes at a time.)

A *good way to start* is to roll off morning stiffness. That means you get on the bike every day. Exercising for 10 or 12 minutes is enough to get the juices going but not enough to suppress the appetite.

For a real workout, start 3 hours after eating a meal.

An *easy 10-minute no-sweat rolling session* can take the place of an after-dinner stroll.

WARMUP

Exercise stresses your body. Warming up is a way of preparing your body for this stress. Exercise raises your internal temperature and cardiac output. Warming up makes this increase gradual. Sudden effort and cold strain the heart, muscles, tendons and joints. Warming up helps prevent strain, muscle tears, soreness and exercise-induced heart attacks.

Even moderate exercise triples the amount of blood pushed out by the heart when you're resting. The blood is also redistributed from the interior of the body to the muscles. You want to have this happen gradually.

They say that you're not going aerobic until you sweat, and when you're sweating you can consider that you're warmed up.

There are two kinds of warmup: passive and active. Passive includes clothes, massage, liniment, baths and showers. (Casey Stengel said Satchel Paige took long hot showers before he pitched—and he pitched into his sixties.)

Active warmup usually means doing the target exercise at a lower level of intensity. But it can mean "jangling around gently as you move," as Satchel said.

Stretching is someplace in between. It should not, as many people think, be done as part of a warmup. Stretching your muscles before they are warmed up can cause tears. Save stretching for after your cycling session.

Passive Warmup

Wear your hat or a sweatband; you lose an astonishing amount of heat through your scalp; there are lots of blood vessels there; that's why you bleed like a pig from a scalp cut.

Nifty bike racers' hats only cost a few dollars; and you can build up your nerve to wear one outside on a bike ride by getting used to the feel.

Sweatbands, bike hats or, better yet, a woolen watch cap will help you warm up. Three quarters of our energy is spent making heat, so when you're warming up—you're warming up.

A windbreaker or a warmup top may shorten the 10% or 20% of your workout that should be spent warming up. If you've ever watched a track meet, you'll notice that athletes wear warmup suits until the last minute, and put them back on as soon as they stop running or jumping; they're trying to conserve body heat and prevent injuries.

Just because warmup suits are a good idea, doesn't mean rubber exercise suits are recommended; those are invitations to hyperthermia or heat exhaustion. You don't want to cut off the possibility of the sweat evaporating. Sweat cools you as it evaporates and limits the amount you can heat up.

Active Warmup

You want to start slowly, with a good rhythm. Nice and easy does it; never go hard at the start, thinking that will get you warmed up faster; until you warm up, going hard will be anerobic, not aerobic, so it won't help you get fit anyway.

Start with the resistance off or very low and slowly raise it to the point where you normally use it. On a wind-load machine, start at a lower gear than your cruising gear.

Start pedaling at about 40rpms and try to keep it up as long as possible...a minute or two. Work physiologists discovered that pedaling or walking downstairs at a rate below one's normal walking speed is as much work as going at or above this speed because the oxygen turnover increases.

Pedal slowly and evenly. This ensures that blood fills the muscles evenly. Don't push hard on the pedals.

At the point when you start to sweat, most of your blood has moved from your body core to your muscles.

Your heart rate will probably be at 60% of maximum.

When you have started sweating, you are burning energy at five to six calories a minute.

It can take a while to work up to a sweat. Don't try to rush it.

ROLLDOWN

A rolldown is just as important as a warmup. That is because it is just as much of a strain on your body to stop suddenly as it is to start suddenly.

Going from a sprint to a total halt is very stressful to your heart. Your blood pressure plummets; it drops so low that it can cause fainting and irregular heartbeats.

Doctors at Harvard Medical School found that this happened even with healthy young men and suggested that the best strategy would be for the work load to be diminished gradually.

Rolling down slowly removes the lactic acid that has accumulated in the muscles. It is removed more quickly by light exercise than by rest. So a gradual slowdown helps prevent muscle soreness.

The rolldown is the warmup in reverse. About 5 or 10 minutes before you want to stop, lessen the resistance or go into a lower gear. Work at the lower intensity for 3 to 5 minutes, then start slowing down the pedal revs. For the last minute or so, pedal more slowly than you can walk—at about 40 revs a minute.

Now do your stretching. It will help prevent muscle soreness as it washes out the lactic acid. If you are limber, there is probably no need to stretch.

Don't take a shower or bath immediately after

you exercise. Wait until at least 10 minutes after you have stopped sweating. Otherwise you will put undue stress on your heart.

LAYOFFS

Sometimes life gets complicated and you have to break training. Illness, injury, business, family —all can keep you from sticking to your exercise routine.

You lose about half of the benefits of your last session in a week to ten days. You lose the rest over about three months, so how much conditioning you lose depends on how long you've had to lay off and how long you've been training.

If you stop for three or four days after only exercising for a week, you have to start over. If you take a longer warmup and rolldown, you might be able to stay on the same amount of time as your last workout.

After 3½ weeks (lots of people have overdone it and quit by this point) you're just beginning to feel better and are tempted to overdo it—then you *have* to lay off.

If you're suffering from overtraining effects there's a tendency to give yourself a present of a few days off. You've only lost about a week's conditioning.

Don't try to start again at the very same level. Start with an easy workout and take a very long warmup.

Take your pulse and listen to your body talk to regain lost shape. The aerobic endurance has gone down but there's still some training effect, so the legs are still strong. The danger is using up the whole day in a half-hour workout.

But if one workout forces you to become part of the couch, it makes it even harder to get on again. So the first day's easy workout with the long warmup and the hunting for a proper cadence and resistance should be followed the next day by another one just like it.

AEROBIC TRAINING

At rest we burn two thirds fat, and the oxygen we breathe burns with glycogen (our stored sugar).

As we become more active, we burn less fat and more oxygen with glycogen.

By the time we've gone aerobic and started sweating, we're burning mostly oxygen and glycogen.

Stored in the muscles is energy that can be burned without oxygen. The body uses this energy to make rapid movements like jumping and sprinting. It's what gets you out of danger before you have time to think about it.

When we use this energy, lactic acid—which shuts down the muscles—builds up. It is this lactic acid that causes muscle pain.

As you tap this anerobic (without oxygen) energy, you start to build up an oxygen debt.

This is why you're out of breath from running upstairs or trying to catch a bus when you've gone faster than you can—that is, beyond your aerobic level.

Spent aerobic energy stresses the body system to gain endurance, so that until you reach a high level some of your workout is bound to be anerobic.

All muscle pain is not caused by lactic acid buildup but may be caused by tears and bruises.

Sprinting is purely anerobic; running the mile is half anerobic and half aerobic.

Anerobic energy builds up slowly; and a hard workout can drain off a large amount of this energy. It can take up to two days to build up again. So, besides the body's general need to recover from the new stresses caused by your workout sessions, this is the basis of the hard-easy day training theory.

Some physical training programs offer the shortcut of going hard: 10 minutes at 80% instead of 20 or 25 at 70%. This is a poor idea because the harder effort calls for both a longer warmup and a longer rolldown, so the time saved isn't much, considering the chance of overdoing and all that lactic acid pain.

The anerobic sprinting energy system is trained along with the aerobic one. You may still be out of breath after running up the stairs after the training effect starts in six or eight weeks—but you've gotten stronger and gone up the stairs faster. You recover faster from your oxygen debt, yet your perceived exertion is the same.

Interval training alternates hard effort with rest periods of light effort. Lactic acid is reduced faster by light effort than by rest, which is why a sprint finish to a workout is no good and an adequate rolldown is a necessity.

The walk-run-walk alternation of the beginning jogger shows that, by using the stored anerobic energy, the increased oxygen turnover of the effort allows energy to increase and training to take place. Alternating fast and slow pedaling allows you to build up your cycling time.

At over 60% to 70% of the aerobic capacity, lactic acid increases with effort. When the lactic acid level is high enough, muscular contraction is slowed. Lactic acid can actually shut down the muscle cells. Fatigue, pain or an attack of the slows results. This can be dramatic—a sudden pitching of the sprinting runner onto the track; the forcing of the distance runner to drop out. On a bike, there's no need to stop—the fatigue of the muscles forces a slowdown, and continual light effort reduces the lactic acid buildup.

As your aerobic capacity increases, you produce less lactic acid. You have less need to tap anerobic energy or are budgeting it better.

After a hard effort the demand for energy drops but the oxygen demand continues.

The "oxygen debt" is not to repay the oxygen used but to increase the production of chemicals used by the muscles and to rid the muscles of the lactic acid built up.

INCREASING YOUR WORKOUT

Extending the time gradually is the simplest way of gaining endurance. Don't try to increase the load until you can cycle for at least 20 minutes.

If you can get on the bike, do a good warmup, start sweating and keep it up for 8, 10, 12 minutes, you're really on your way to building aerobic endurance.

Your goal should be to extend the length of the aerobic—sweaty—part of your workout until it is at least 20 minutes long.

Be Systematic

If you're having difficulty increasing the time and think that you should be making more progress, what you can do is use a more systematic workout—the kind track racers do.

Divide the workout into two equal parts. If you can do 10 minutes, do a 5-minute work interval followed by a minute or so of easy pedaling and then another 5-minute work interval, ending with a short controlled "sprint for your life" effort. (This is not quite as hard as you can go or anywhere near as hard as you could go if you were showing off.) Check that your heart rate has stayed below 80% during this maximum effort.

When sprinting, take at least 10 seconds to come up to speed and don't try to hold your maximum speed for more than 10 seconds. Then roll evenly down to cruising speed and start your rolldown.

If this sprinting feels uncomfortable, replace it with a longer interval of 20 to 30 seconds of hard pedaling. It may take a while until any type of rapid pedaling feels right.

Don't Stop Abruptly

Over five work sessions, increase the time of the first interval to about 7 minutes. Increase the easy-rolling recovery time if necessary. If you are having trouble doing your second 5-minute interval, you have increased the time too much.

If you are doing six workouts a week, skip the finish sprint on your easy days.

When your recovery rate from the first interval is a minute or less (check that your heart rate is down to 60% to 65%), you can start increasing the time of your second interval.

Try to pedal evenly and smoothly. If you start to drift slowly down in pedal revs, don't correct yourself by pedaling rapidly but get up to speed evenly. This sounds minor, only the difference of a few seconds, but a rapid increase in pedaling speed draws on your anerobic reserve, makes the heart rate rise rapidly, and that demands another slowing down to rest from that.

Uneven pedaling produces more uneven pedaling. The smoother and more evenly you can pedal, the better.

When you are up to 15 minutes of aerobic work, you can go back to your 5-minute standard ride—for your first interval—so that you're doing three 5-minute intervals with about a minute of easy pedaling in between, with as much rest as is necessary to complete the third interval.

Over five to ten sessions, try to eliminate the rest period beween the second and third intervals. Use your "sprint for your life" at the end of the third interval and monitor how this feels.

On a hard-easy day schedule, the rolldown should be longer on the hard day.

If you have trouble keeping your heart rate up in the 70% to 75% training zone, start out by dividing the workout into three or four sessions and push pretty hard during each of them—not as hard as you do for your "sprint for your life" but hard enough so that you know you're working. Work toward a recovery time of under a minute.

Being able to do your next workout is more important than pushing yourself to keep a training schedule.

So listen to your body talk. Are you able to breathe without panting? Can you talk? Are your arms relaxed, not gripping the handlebars too tightly?

INTERVAL TRAINING

If you're making progress with your endurance training and would like to be able to "go faster," you can do an occasional interval training session. Athletes on a six-day hard-easy training schedule usually do one day of sprint training to build up speed.

Managing an interval training session means using your heart rate to tell you how hard to go.

Short spurts, under 30 seconds long, increase the ability of the muscles to take up energy without overstressing their capacity to deal with the lactic acid. After about 5 minutes of light work between sprints, the batteries are recharged and ready for another go. With training, the rest periods can be cut and the anerobic capacity increased.

Just going at it hard for a long time is not interval training, because the only rest interval is when you stop.

There is about 10 seconds of all-out energy available, so that a short sprint on a bike (you want to wind up evenly to maximum effort and then wind down from that) permits about 15 seconds of extremely high speed revs.

Rest Cycle

With short intervals, you rest three to four times the length of the interval. A trained athlete might do as many as five sets of eight to ten repetitions.

You want to get the heart beat down to below 75% of your maximum heart rate, and to 60% to 65% between sets.

You are building up to longer intervals: 4 minutes of effort and 4 minutes of rest repeated three times are what you're working for; 6 minutes would be 3 minutes in between, and 8 minutes would be 2½ minutes in between.

The rest at an aerobic level permits a larger flow of blood to reach the muscles (stroke volume). More work can be performed at a higher intensity than by going steadily at a particular speed.

There is a tendency during a session to try to extend the maximum effort instead of breaking it up into smaller segments. Exercise physiologists have found that the latter results in greater overall endurance.

Any sprinter starts out by needing 6 minutes to recover from a 10-second all-out effort. By continually stressing at near maximum effort, he or she is able to string out a long series of repeats.

You have to use your pulse rate to manage any interval training program.

Intervals are hard and there is a definite risk of muscle and joint injury.

WEIGHT TRAINING

Indoor bicycle endurance training goes together perfectly with low-weight, high-repetition weight training—but not at the same time.

Biking while lifting weights is a terrible idea. Alternating the two activities is the way to go. Build your aerobic capacity three days a week with a cycling workout and build your strength three days a week with a session of weight training.

In order for bones to stay strong they have to be weight-bearing, which is why swimming, while very good for your cardiovascular health, really doesn't help prevent osteoporosis.

If you run out of leg strength before you run out of air, leg lifts with light weights will help you build the cycling muscles.

Running and skiing give you a cardiovascular workout faster than biking because, until you get used to cycling, your upper body is very tight. That limits the circulation of the blood.

This might suggest that you use combination rowing and cycling machines; unfortunately, that slows down the cycling motion by making you shift your hips.

It is thought that the longevity of orchestra conductors is partially due to the free motion of the arms, so there may not be a need for weights to help build upper body strength. And older people who practice Tai Chi, the Chinses slow-motion calisthenics, have 70% of the aerobic capacity of much younger trained runners.

Skilled cyclists hang loose and make lots of minor adjustments to keep blood from pooling, or they minimize the possibility by changing their position, putting their hands on different parts of the handlebars. During the rolldown after a race they also occasionally sit up and stretch.

Many exercise programs alternate a day of cardiovascular work with a day of strength training. But weight lifting should be learned under the supervision and monitoring of someone knowledgeable. It is very easy to injure yourself.

Weight training coach Bob Pearl says you should never try to lift weights while bicycling or running. Running with weights throws you off balance, your elbows whip and you can get tendonitis. If you are strengthening the upper body, then the lower body should not be moving but should act as a base, and vice versa.

Since it is difficult to set new habits, we think a class at a gym or Y where you can get the supervision you need for lifting weights is a good investment in health.

ADAPTING TO HEAT AND COLD

ACCLIMATIZATION

A wonderful by-product of training is the better ability of the body to deal with both heat and cold. The improved circulation both gets rid of heat more efficiently to cool you and produces it better when needed to keep you warm.

You can turn the thermostat down a little or do without so much air conditioning. Sudden 20- or 30-degree changes in the weather won't affect you as strongly.

At rest, heat is produced by the organs inside us: the works—the liver, kidneys, heart and brain. During exercise, it's produced by the muscles. The blood is cooled or warmed as it goes through the various parts of the body. The skin temperature is always slightly lower.

Feeling hot or cold depends on skin temperature, and the comfort range is very small. When it's above 93° F. we begin to feel warm; below 91.5° F. we begin to feel cool.

Temperature sensation is comparative rather than absolute. If you put one hand in cold water and the other in hot water and then put both in lukewarm water, the water will feel cold to the hand that was in hot water and hot to the hand that was in cold water. Similarly, 50° F. almost always feels cold at the beginning of fall and warm at the end of winter.

When you are in good physical shape, you adapt better to both heat and cold.

Heat

If you're planning to go to a hot climate on vacation, you will enjoy it a whole lot more if you first get acclimated to heat—and stationary bicycling is the perfect aerobic exercise for heat adaptation.

Riding a stationary bicycle seems like hot and sweaty work compared to riding a bicycle outdoors. That's because when you're outdoors the extra heat is stripped off as you move through the air. But in either case about three quarters of the energy you produce by turning the pedals is burned in the form of heat.

As you gain aerobic capacity you will be able to deal with this heat better and get more work done at the same time; this is because the exercise is acclimatizing you to heat.

Adapting to heat takes four to seven days; four days for the fit, longer for the out of shape.

No sweating occurs until the body temperature reaches a certain level, which is called the set point. The higher temperature can come from the air outside the body or from the exercise done by the body.

In both acclimatization and training, the amount of sweat and blood increases and the kidney temperature and heart rate go down. More blood flows to the skin and less to the kidneys.

Once acquired, acclimatization is retained for two weeks or more. The longer you work at the higher temperature, the better the adaptation to heat. Proof of a training effect is that the heart slows down and the body temperature drops.

Dehydration

Both the increased sweat and the increased blood volume that result from adapting to heat depend on drinking lots of water.

Acclimatized people can take the heat better because they are less likely to become dehydrated. Their sweat has a lower concentration of salt (the same amount dissolved in a larger volume of water). This makes the cells give up water and the nerves flash thirst cues. Since the people feel thirstier, they drink more. And that's the only way to maintain correct water balance.

Replace Salt

If you want something salty after you've sweated for an hour or so, don't deny this impulse. Have a pretzel or add a pinch of salt to the water you drink. Salt hunger is innate in mammals and disappears when the lack is filled.

Cold

You don't really adapt to the cold quite the way you do to the heat. That's why there are houses and clothing. Good blood circulation certainly helps, as it does in any stress adaptation.

Good physical condition, good circulation, and a good warmup are especially important if you have to work or want to play hard in the cold.

When it's cold, the body conserves heat to keep the inner organs warm by taking it from the arms and legs. The cold makes muscles shorten, which makes injury more likely. Furthermore, cold hands and feet are clumsy hands and feet. This is because the circulation of blood is decreased.

When your circulation has been improved through a program of indoor cycling, you can do your usual amount of work without putting as great a strain on your heart or your muscles and tendons.

Both increased metabolism and increased insulation help you get used to the cold. Increased insulation is body fat or extra clothing.

Many people gain weight during the winter. That's because eating raises body temperature and makes you feel warmer. So they eat more and exercise less. Exercise also raises body temperature, so indoor cycling is a good way to keep the extra pounds from creeping up on you. If you ate and exercised the same way during the winter as you did during the rest of the year, you would actually lose weight. Canadian soldiers do, Dr. Roy Shepherd found out at the Toronto School of

Physical Health Foundation. A lab experiment confirmed this: men lost much more weight when they exercised in a cold chamber than in a warm one.

What does this teach weight-conscious Americans? Get the increased metabolism from indoor cycling, but get the added insulation from clothing. Cycling (and cross-country skiing) clothes make lots of sense, since they were developed to let you exercise and stay fairly dry even on the coldest days.

A very good use of a stationary bike is to warm up for work outside in the snow and cold.

You can exercise in an almost unheated room, put on another layer when you cool down, and just add a windbreaker to go outdoors. You lessen the shock to your cardiovascular system by not going from a very hot to a very cold place.

SWEATING

Why You Need Extra Water When You Exercise

You breathe more frequently, exhaling more water vapor.

Your body temperature rises. Sweating dissipates the heat—it is your built-in air conditioner.

Water is released when you break down fat molecules and proteins.

"Exercise dehydrates the body," says Dr. Mondenard, physician to the cyclists of the Tour de France. "A feeling of thirst only appears when perspiration loss is over a half liter [pint] an hour, too late to reestablish fluid balance. So it is fundamental during physical effort to drink without being thirsty, that is to say, to drink systematically before feeling the need for it."

Okay, How Much Water?

Individual needs depend on body size, metabolism rate, physical activity and climate. Any liquid will do: coffee, tea, beer, soups and sodas are all mostly water. But only one liquid is calorie-free, caffeine-free and almost sodium-free: water.

When exercising: a cup for every 15 minutes you exercise.

The rest of the time: 6 to 8 cups besides what you get in your food (vegetables and fruits are about 75% water, meat and fish 50%). More if the temperature is above 75° F.

Important: Cool water is absorbed more quickly than hot water. You can only absorb about 12 ounces a half hour, so you should start drinking water *before* you exercise. If you're going really hard or it's a hot day, you're losing more than you can absorb. And on a dry day you may not even notice it.

Electrolyte Replacement Needed?

Not really. Both sugar and potassium slow the absorption of liquid from the stomach, and you don't want that to happen. If you feel very washed out from sweating on a very hot day, you might have a little orange juice or Gatorade. But they are both too concentrated: dilute juice by half, and use 1 measure of Gatorade to 2 of water.

What About Salt?

There is three times more salt in the blood than in sweat, so the concentration of salt in the body actually goes up when we sweat. That's

SWEAT IS BEAUTIFUL. When exercising, sweat usually means you've entered the training zone. Be sure to wait until you've stopped sweating to take a shower. CAUTION: Wear no clothing that inhibits evaporation such as rubberized suits.

what triggers the "thirsty" alarm. Doctors recommend salting food a little more than usual on hot days or after heavy exercise. They don't approve of salt tablets because these overload the system and actually make you lose more salt; they also cause abdominal upsets.

Why You Must Sweat

All vigorous exercise raises your temperature. Sweating cools you down. It's your built-in air conditioner and keeps you from overheating.

There is little aerobic benefit until you sweat. And this does not happen until the body temperature reaches a certain set point.

Indoor biking makes you sweat profusely. You will seem to sweat more than when you bike outdoors because, when the bike moves through the air, the air dries the sweat on your body. This evaporation is what cools you. One reason why high humidity combined with high heat is so dangerous is that it makes evaporation more difficult.

To assure evaporation while cycling indoors, open the top and bottom of windows to create a cross current of air and/or use a window fan or the air conditioner on the fan setting.

Dehydration

Dehydration reduces heat tolerance. Dehydration reduces plasma volume when you can least tolerate it. One of the reasons the excitant drugs

are so dangerous is that they dehydrate.

Water deficits as low as 1% to 2% of body weight cause measurable evidence of increased circulatory strain as indicated by increases in heart rates and rectal temperatures.

When there is a 1% to 8% reduction in body weight from dehydration, most of this is in blood volume; in fact, reductions in circulating plasma volume are two and a half times the proportional loss of body weight.

A 10% loss of body fluid is serious; 20% is fatal. At 8000 feet as little as a 3% loss is serious.

Unfortunately, even acclimatized people exercising in the heat (as opposed to resting) only drink about half to a third as much water as they lose in sweat. Serious dehydration, with circulatory strain and overheating, may result.

The Thirst Idea You Should Have

Forced drinking of water is the only way to prevent dehydration when exercising strenuously.

"Drink before you are thirsty" is an old cyclist saying. It's good advice because our body doesn't do a very good job of telling us that it is time to drink something, particularly when it's hot or we are working hard. This defect increases with age.

About 2½ quarts of water are lost and replaced every day in an average adult. Individual needs depend on body size, metabolism rate, physical activity and climate.

Yet the kidneys regulate water balance so perfectly that water loss equals water gain.

Normal Water Loss

Nearly 2 cups of water normally leave through the skin every day—and that's without sweating. The outer layers of the skin must be kept moist, so minimize the use of antiperspirants.

The lungs: another 2 cups a day leave when you breathe. Each time you breathe out, you're breathing out water vapor. So the more often you have to breathe the more water you lose through your lungs. And exercise makes you breathe more often.

If you combine exercise with high altitude, you can really get dehydrated. In a day of mountain climbing you can lose several quarts of water through your lungs.

Feces: 1 or 2 cups of water are normally excreted. Which explains why the main danger in diarrhea is dehydration, as normal water loss is greatly multiplied. On the other hand, if you get constipated after a few days of indoor cycling, it is a sign of chronic dehydration.

Habitual low-level dehydration results in problems with almost every part of the body, from blood, to kidney, to lung, to colon, to bones and joints, since water is necessary to practically every function.

Signs of Dehydration:

- dizziness
- rapid breathing
- muscle cramps
- fever
- drowsiness
- unconsciousness
- death

Signs of Heat Exhaustion:

- weakness
- pale, moist skin
- nausea
- dizziness

First Aid: Lie down, then sip diluted juice or salty broth.

Signs of Heat Stroke:

- flushed, dry skin
- fever
- delirium

This is a medical emergency: Get cool inside and out immediately! Surround with ice, force cold water down, get medical help.

FEVER FIGHTS INFECTION

There's been some recent research that suggests that one reason exercise helps keep you healthy and even cures you of illnesses is because it raises your temperature.

Fever is an important part of the body's immune response to infection, helping prevent its spread throughout the body. It triggers the production of antibodies, the proliferation of white blood corpuscles, and stimulates helper T-cells to start a direct attack on invaders. Antibiotics work best at fever temperature in part because fever deprives bacteria of the iron that they need.

Fever also encourages the production of interferon to fight viruses. One study compared patients with colds who were given aspirin, which lowers the temperature, to patients who were given a placebo. The patients who received aspirin shed more viruses, which proved that they were more infectuous and that their colds weren't under control.

So the old-time bike riders who recommended "rolling away a cold" were right—the raised temperature of the exercise did just that.

Recently, at the University of Michigan Medical School, it was shown that an hour of pedaling on a stationary bicycle released a substance into the blood that caused fever when injected into laboratory rats.

But Michigan's Dr. Matthew J. Kluger noted that, "For each degree rise in Centigrade temperature, the body's metabolic rate increases about 10 percent: heart rate, respiration, all the metabolic functions are speeded up."

So you have to decide whether or not you want to experiment on yourself; conventional wisdom advises you not to exercise when you're sick, but to rest until you're well.

If you do decide to exercise, monitor your heart rate carefully. Each degree of fever increases the heart rate about ten beats, and any real effort can send it soaring over the target rate into the danger zone.

Cruising along at 50% to 60% of your maximum heart rate will still help the blood circulate and reduce the pain that comes with fever when you get a cold.

Old-time athletes always felt the first signs of disease were a signal to go ahead and try to stave it off by getting on their bikes.

DIET AND EXERCISE

EXERCISE AND DIET

The Perfect Marriage for Trim Bodies

Study after study has shown that the main difference between obese and normal people is how much they exercise, not how much they eat.

In one study obese women ate the same amount at three energy-expenditure levels—and the more they exercised the more weight they burned off; normal-weight women ate more when they exercised more and didn't gain or lose weight.

If you reduce the amount you eat without also exercising, your body will soon adjust to the lower calorie intake by slowing down. Only exercise can overcome this set point and keep your metabolism rate high.

You are burning fat at a 12% to 15% higher rate for from an hour to four hours after you exercise. Furthermore, exercise protects your heart both by lowering the total amount of cholesterol in your blood and by increasing the healthful HDL type.

Calories Used in Movement

You are always burning some calories: 50–75 calories an hour sleeping and up to 90 calories an hour eating or watching TV. If you balance your intake and your output, you should stay the same weight.

As you warm up, you burn about 6 calories a minute.

If you do 12mph on a 3-speed bike you are working as hard as if you run a mile in 12 minutes —about 600 calories an hour. On an indoor bike or on a 10-speed with a wind-load simulator this is about 15 to 16 miles an hour. If you can keep this up for a half hour with your heart rate somewhere between the 70% and 80% level, you will have run the equivalent of 2½ miles and will have burned 300 calories.

Set Realistic Goals About Weight

There are enough people arguing about weight tables without our adding any fuel to the subject. Once you start getting a training effect from exercise you will have a better idea of how you feel about your body weight. Do nothing drastic one way or the other—two pounds a month is a difference of 200 calories a day—easy to manage with some added exercise. If you added 200 calories of exercise and ate 200 calories a day less, you would lose a pound a week.

Except when it turns cold. Your body loses less water through evaporation then, so you automatically weigh more. If you experience a weight gain that you can't explain, check the weather.

Just Losing Weight Shouldn't Be Your Goal!

The scale can be misleading. How much you weigh is only a rough reflection of how fit you are. As you exercise, you may not lose weight—but you will lose fat. Lean muscle weighs more than fat, and when you exercise, you are replacing fat with muscle. For someone who is really fat, losing about 25% of the fat will increase aerobic capacity by over 10%.

Dieting without exercise seldom works and may endanger your health. Getting and keeping aerobic endurance is just as important as having an adequate diet.

Soon science may be able to control the fat storage cycle. But until then exercise is the only way to burn off fat.

Being overweight is a problem if it slows you down, makes you feel uncomfortable or raises your blood pressure.

Getting strong will make you feel better about yourself and make it easier to do what needs to be done.

Ordinarily that's much more important than what the scale says.

The mirror and the way your clothes fit will be saying nice things long before the scale does.

Worry About Fat, Not Weight

Most people know if they are carrying extra fat around, and exercise will reduce the amount whether you know how much that is or not.

If you want to figure out what percentage of your body is fat rather than muscle, a simple way of figuring it out is the "jiggle test." Stand in front of a mirror; jump up and down. Everything that jiggles is fat.

For greater accuracy, athletes get weighed underwater; that way the coaches can figure out what percentage of an athlete's body weight is fat. Fit women range between 18% and 22% fat; fit men between 15% and 19%.

If you want to try to figure it out for yourself, you can buy a "pinch" caliper like the Fat-o-Meter. Getting one of these could make you the life of the party. It comes with very complete instructions for measuring fat at different places on the body and formulas for figuring out what percentage of your body is fat rather than muscle. However, it takes quite a bit of practice to do this accurately. If you're going to use the results as a reason to go on a diet or to monitor your exercise program, the measurements should be done at a gym or clinic by someone who has experience in using such a gadget.

Why Ups and Downs in Weight Are Dangerous and Self-Defeating

When humans or lab animals, lean or fat, are starved, their blood pressure, blood sugar and cholesterol fall almost immediately.

When weight is regained, blood pressure, blood sugar and cholesterol skyrocket far above the original levels, putting a terrific strain on the cardiovascular system.

Each time you diet, you teach the body how to get along on less weight, according to Kelly Brownell of the University of Pennsylvania. Many women who attended his weight loss clinic did not lose weight, even though they were only eating 600 to 700 calories a day. "These tended to be women who had dieted frequently in the past," Brownell said.

Brownell and his colleages tested their hypothesis on rats by making them obese and then putting them on a diet. Then the test was done again, giving them "precisely the same amount of · food to the gram." The first time they dieted, the rats lost their excess weight in 21 days and regained it in 46 days. The second time, it took them 46 days to lose the extra weight and only 14 days to regain it!

Don't Starve Your Body with Too Few Calories

Some athletes starve their hearts by eating too little food to support the amount of exercise they're getting. "Nutritional arrhythmia" was the explanation given for the death of twelve marathoners; all were at or near their lowest adult body weight, and all were on severely restricted diets.

Sports for which weight classifications are important, such as wrestling and boxing, have also encouraged dangerous diet restrictions. Many adolescents are so concerned with not being fat that they combine diet and purging to endanger their health. Indoor cycling can help them control their weight and stay healthy.

When to Eat: New and Un-American

(Though the French have been doing it for years).

25% Calories at breakfast
50% At lunch
25% At supper

In order to minimize fat storage, some scientists are suggesting a radical change in American dietary patterns: either eat most of your calories at breakfast and lunch rather than at dinner or else eat many smaller meals throughout the day.

We tend to side with those suggesting more small meals because energy, blood sugar and insulin levels will be more stable, more of the food is likely to be used up instead of being stored as fat, and it is easier on the stomach and digestive system. On the other hand, it may be harder to control your fat intake this way.

In either case, exercise lightly after you eat to burn off extra calories. A small snack right after exercise may help keep you from eating a whole lot later. It takes a few minutes for you to feel full after you've eaten something, so waiting between courses at a large meal helps cut down on the total amount eaten.

Heart Disease Risk Factors

(From the federally financed Framingham Heart Study)
1. Heredity
2. Body type
3. Cigarette smoking
4. High blood pressure
5. High cholesterol level
6. Obesity
7. Diabetes
8. Stress ("type A" behavior)
9. Inactivity

With a prudent combination of exercise and diet you can lower six of the nine risk factors.

WHAT TO EAT

"In many cases you can reduce your disease risk as soon as you adopt good nutrition habits—even if you adopt these habits at 60," says Dr. George Bray of the University of Southern California.

The American Heart Association recommends that 50% of your total calories come from complex carbohydrates, 20% from protein, 30% from fat.

This diet is no different from that prescribed for Olympic athletes: low in protein, low in fat, high in complex carbohydrates, and supplemented with lots and lots of water. Such a diet helps prevent heart disease, cancer and diabetes. An added benefit is that your appetite is satisfied with less calories.

Protein

Protein is essential to build and repair body tissues, but, except for the elderly, most of us eat too much of it. Six ounces a day, preferably some with each meal, is enough for a 170-pound grown man. If you are ill, still growing, pregnant or lactating, you need more. But excercise itself does not increase your need for it; exercise uses carbohydrates and fat as fuel. You can't eat animal protein without eating a lot of saturated fat.

81

Blood Sugar

When the level of sugar in the blood goes up, insulin is released to bring it back to normal. This does four things: (1) raises the blood level of triglycerides, implicated in heart disease; (2) encourages the storage of calories as fat; (3) makes us hungry again quickly; (4) releases serotonin, which makes us sleepy.

You want the level to go up as slowly as possible to minimize these effects. Of all carbohydrates, those that raise it least are oatmeal, pasta and lentils.

Lowering Fat and Cholesterol Levels

The body needs some fat for proper functioning and to transport vitamins A, D, E, and K, which are only soluble in fat. Twenty percent of fat in the diet is safe; over 30% strains the heart.

The liver produces about 1000 milligrams of cholesterol every day; these are essential to the production of cell membranes, nerve fiber sheaths, vitamin D and sex hormones. Cholesterol circulates in the blood in globular particles of low-density lipoprotein (LDL). These are removed from the blood when they are taken up by cells that extract from it the cholesterol they need.

When a cell has all the cholesterol it needs, it makes fewer LDL receptors. A reduction in the number of receptors leads to a rise in the blood level of LDL—and to atherosclerosis.

An atherosclerotic plaque is formed when LDL invades the wall of an artery and deposits its cholesterol.

The HDL Cholesterol Story

It is not enough to know your total cholesterol figure, however; you also have to know its ratio to HDL (high-density lipoprotein). This ratio is the best predictor of future coronary heart disease, according to Dr. William P. Castelli, director of the Framingham Heart Study. The lower the ratio the better: it is normally below 5 for men, below 4 for women.

Whereas LDL forms plaques, HDL removes them. So you want to increase the number of HDLs and decrease the number of LDLs. Some medical researchers feel that only the amount of HDL is important.

Aerobic exercise increases HDLs—even modest exercise, like 20 minutes a day of indoor cycling. Beta antagonists like brethine (for asthma) and dilantin (for epilepsy) also raise HDLs.

Cigarette smoking, birth control pills and beta blockers lower HDLs.

Restricting fat intake and losing weight decreases LDLs. So does medication prescribed for this purpose.

Cholesterol in Food

Cholesterol is only found in animal foods. But any saturated fat raises the cholesterol level in the blood. Saturated fats are not needed in the diet. Polyunsaturates supply the three essential dietary fatty acids and can transport fat-soluble vitamins.

Dietary Fiber

A high-fiber diet reduced some patients' blood cholesterol by as much as 25% over several months; it stabilized blood sugar levels enough to eliminate the need for insulin injections for two thirds of patients who developed diabetes as adults; it eliminated symptoms in many patients with diverticulosis, spastic and irritable bowels and chronic constipation.

Soluble fiber, like the pectin in apples, dissolves in water to form a kind of jelly. Other fibers, like those in oats, corn, beans and seeds, form gums. Insoluble fiber, like the bran in wheat, does not dissolve in water but absorbs it like a sponge.

Fiber works by slowing absorption. Pectin will form a jelly in the stomach; this releases more slowly into the small intestine than fruit juice and avoids a sudden rush of sugar, thereby helping stabilize the blood sugar level. Other fibers trap fat, cholesterol and bile and carry them beyond the small intestine, where they pass out of the body.

Fiber also moves waste more rapidly through the lower bowel. Scientists believe bacteria in your colon turn undigested fats into carcinogens; these chemicals then work on the colon cells and turn them cancerous. By cutting both the amount of time these bacteria have to work and the amount of time the chemicals touch the walls of the colon, dietary fiber helps protect against colon cancer.

All fruits and vegetables, all whole-grain cereals and all legumes (beans, peanuts, peas) contain dietary fiber. The fiber in carrots, oatmeal and chickpeas is particularly effective in lowering cholesterol. Pure bran may carry vitamins and minerals out of the body along with the cholesterol.

Avoiding Dietary Carcinogens

You can't avoid them all! Vegetables don't want to be eaten and protect themselves with natural pesticides that resist insect and fungal invasion and can cause cancer in animals. Scientists estimate that we eat several grams of these natural pesticides a day—thousands of times as much as man-made pesticides.

We've all learned to avoid nitrosamines in smoked or salt-cured food; but there are other cancer-causing substances you can avoid: rancid oils and fats; burned and browned particles formed by heating protein during cooking— whether charred meat or toast; and mold-contaminated foods.

The body has many defense mechanisms against carcinogens, including continuous shedding of the surface layer of the skin, stomach, cornea, intestines and colon. Many enzymes also protect cells from damage, as does uric acid, a strong antioxidant; a low uric acid level may be a risk factor in cigarette-caused cancer.

The fruits, vegetables and grains that form the complex carbohydrates of the prudent diet contain the following antioxidants: vitamin C, vitamin E, beta-carotene (which the body converts to vitamin A), selenium, and glutathione. Vegetables in the cabbage family (cauliflower, broccoli, brussels sprouts, kale, turnips) seem to have some special ability to inhibit carcinogenesis.

Potassium

Exercise is going to make you sweat more; and if you sweat very heavily you may need extra potassium, a crucial regulator of the amount of water in cells that also catalyzes the release of energy from food. Bike riders stock up on bananas and oranges. Peanut butter, potatoes and coffee are also good sources of potassium.

Sodium

Salt has certainly had a bad rap from doctors. Yet salt deficiency is possible when excess sweating is combined with a vegetarian diet (plants store little or no sodium); muscle aches, cramps and weakness follow. A very small amount of salt (1/4 teaspoon) can cure the deficiency very quickly.

Dr. Derek Denton, probably the world's foremost authority on salt use, has been studying salt appetite for twenty years. His conclusion: salt hunger is a powerful instinct that comes into play the first time a young animal experiences sodium deficiency. Hormones involved in both stress and pregnancy help conserve sodium and stimulate salt appetite; in pregnancy an extra supply is needed for the fetus; stress, sweating and other emergency responses heighten need.

Food or Pills?

Most nutritionists recommend you get your vitamins from food, not pills. Toxic doses of vitamins A and D and of selenium have been reported. It is difficult to get adequate levels of iron and calcium from diets of under 1500 calories without an unacceptably high percentage of fat. We see little harm in a multivitamin-mineral supplement for people at risk.

Eat Fish

Eating fish lowers the risk of heart disease. The University of Leiden in Holland studied a group of middle-aged Dutch males in the town of Zutphen from 1960 to 1980 and found that men who ate only 3 ounces of fish a week had 36% less incidence of heart disease than those who ate no fish.

Men who ate two or three servings a week—between 7 and 11 ounces—had a 64% lower incidence.

DRUGS AND NUTRITION

If you are taking any drug regularly, check to see if it causes nutritional problems and alert your physician.

Examples:

- Antacids deplete phosphate and vitamin D.
- Anticoagulants: avoid liver and leafy green vegetables.
- Anticonvulsants deplete folic acid and limit vitamin D intake.
- Antidiabetic agents (oral) deplete vitamin B_{12}.
- Azulfidine (for colitis) depletes folic acid.
- Colchicine (for gout) inhibits all nutrient absorption plus can deplete vitamin B_{12}.
- Diuretics deplete potassium (often more than can be replaced through diet). You'll feel terribly tired.
- Hydralazine (for high blood pressure) depletes Vitamin B_6.

- INH (for TB) depletes Vitamin B_6.
- Licorice changes electrolyte balance; it should be avoided if you have high blood pressure or colitis.
- Monoamine oxidase (MAO inhibitors): *Avoid all aged and fermented foods* (salamis, cheeses, herring, wines, beers, soy sauces, yogurts) as well as beans, bananas, avocados, beef, liver, cola, chocolate, coffee, raisins, figs.
- Neomycin (antibiotic) depletes vitamin B_{12}.
- Thyroid pills: action inhibited by cabbage family and soybeans.

Don't wash down pills with citric fruit juices or soda without checking with your doctor: the excess acidity can cause some drugs to dissolve in the stomach instead of in the intestines, where they are more readily absorbed into the bloodstream.

SPORTS

PEAKING FOR THE WEEKEND

A sensible training program alternates hard and easy days, but since most of us would like to be able to peak for the weekend instead, we'd like our training program to energize us so we don't spend the weekend lying around and sleeping after our weekly sports spurt.

If you just want to energize yourself so you don't sleep away Sunday, two 20-minute moderate rolling sessions during the week will do as much for your endurance as a half hour of jogging and be a lot less tiring. You can use one of them to suppress the mid-afternoon munchies.

So: rest on Monday, work hard on Tuesday—go almost as hard as you would on the weekend, rest or go lightly on Wednesday, go as hard on Thursday as you did on Tuesday but get some extra sleep, rest or have a light workout on Friday. Tilt the diet toward carbohydrates on Thursday and Friday.

This is a kind of carbo loading. Which does not mean stuffing yourself but just eating more bread and pasta and rice and less fish and other protein sources in your 2400 or whatever your calorie allotment is.

If you've overdone it on Sunday—legs are swollen and achy— a cooldown period, gentle spinning on the cycle for 10 minutes or so, will wash the lactic acid out of your sore muscles and for most people take the place of massage, aspirin and hot bath. If you're recovering from an injury, you may want to add stretches to make bicycling easier for you.

Many of us don't know we've overdone it until Monday morning, of course, when just sitting up in bed can be agony. That same gentle spinning for 10 minutes gets the kinks out easily and more than makes up for the time it takes by getting you smoothly into the week.

If you're a weekend athlete, you've added another risk to the list of eight health-risk factors. "Weekend athletes, those who live a sedentary life, and go and play a tough game of singles, are in the highest risk group," said Paul Dudley White, presidential heart consultant.

If you round out your program with just two indoor cycling sessions during the week, you will cut those risk factors and most likely increase your life expectancy. That's because aerobic exercise lowers the amount of fat under your skin and the cholesterol in your blood. It's also helpful in cutting the bad effects of stress.

You'll also be pleasantly surprised at how much better your game is once you've built some endurance and leg speed through cycling. Professional football, hockey and basketball teams regularly do stationary cycling to help prepare for their strenuous weekends. The coaches know that fatigue plays a big role in injury; the more endurance you have, the less likely you are to be hurt.

Although you will get stronger during the season by just doing what you're doing over the weekends, you gain more endurance by having two other sessions during the week.

CHRONOBIOLOGY FOR THE WEEKEND ATHLETE

Our built-in time clocks, experimenters say, run on a twenty-five-hour day, so on Saturday we sleep an hour longer, and by Sunday night an eleven o'clock bedtime comes at 1 a.m. That's why getting up Monday for a regular nine-to-five workday is very hard.

A good warmup on an indoor bicycle and a high-protein breakfast might just help to start the week.

Prepare for Early Morning Trials

For that big race or meeting or test that's far too early in the morning, when you're suffering from "local jet lag," chronobiology suggests that in three or four days you can reset your energy clock so that you can perform well at 7 or 8 a.m.

Get up earlier each morning; try to do your workout at the same time as the race. Be sure to drink plenty of water before and after exercise during the day. The water balance takes longer than most processes to reset, and if you don't increase your water intake there will be times when body processes will have to slow down; extra water will simply be excreted anyway.

Eat small portions of healthful food and have most of your protein for breakfast or lunch.

If you got up a half hour earlier each day, it shouldn't be too hard to get to bed early the night before.

On race/test/meeting day, have a long early warmup.

Drink coffee or tea the morning of the race, but don't drink any past noon of the day before. This way you utilize caffeine's ability to make the muscles drain off stored energy, and increase your system's ability to get at and use the stored sugar.

If you have your first-, second- and third-day workout earlier than the target time, you can judge how it affects you in order to maximize your performance.

This advice will probably seem naive four or five years from now, when we know a great deal more about the way our biological clocks affect everything from when we take medicine to when we run. Chronobiology is about to start an information revolution in health and medicine. It will be interesting to see how it explains differences between owls (night people) and larks (morning people), and whether these inner clocks can or should be changed.

The Anti-Jet Lag Diet

The Argonne National Laboratory's Anti-Jet Lag Diet alternates feasting "a few thousand calories" with fasting "800 to 1200 calories the second of the four days."

Breakfast and lunch are high-protein to give you fuel to go five or six hours.

High-carbohydrate dinners give you a temporary lift, then drop you down and make it easier to sleep.

The Anti-Jet Lag Diet doesn't change your sleep hours, but uses caffeine, which has been withheld, and a high-protein breakfast on the new local time to reset your built-in time clock.

You can get a wallet-sized plastic-coated card describing the plan more fully by writing to Anti-Jet Lag Diet, OPA, Argonne National Laboratory, 9700 South Cass Avenue, Argonne, IL 60439.

Carbo Loading

Since the aerobic fuel is glycogen, which comes from carbohydrates and sugar, the idea of carbo loading is to make extra glycogen available for a sustained athletic effort, like a marathon or a 100-mile bike ride.

In classic carbohydrate loading, you start one week before making a sustained effort. You deplete the stored energy by a hard workout, eat high-protein meals on Monday, Tuesday and Wednesday, switch over to complete carbohydrate meals Thursday and Friday. You consume about equal amounts of calories each day.

At first it was thought necessary to deplete the system of glycogen early in the week by doing an intense workout followed by a diet high in protein and low in carbohydrates. You were to train fairly lightly on Thursday and Friday, and get your calories from carbohydrates. The same total number of calories were to be consumed each day, only the type of food was different. You then had available an extra supply of glycogen for the Saturday and/or Sunday race.

Some people misunderstood and thought carbo loading was eating twice the normal amount of food like spaghetti and cake, which is lots of fun but bad for the digestive system.

Current thinking doubts the necessity for the depletion phase. For the weekend athlete, whatever you're doing over the weekend is enough depletion. Nowadays physicians frown on any high-cholesterol concentration of fat and protein. Instead, they recommend increasing the carbohydrate content and decreasing the fat and protein content on Thursday and Friday.

BE A BETTER RUNNER

Indoor cycling can improve your running by creating a better balance between the muscles used in running, the muscles used in pushing off and the muscles used in moving the legs between leg strikes.

Besides allowing runners to keep their hard-earned endurance while recovering from running injury, the stationary bicycle will benefit a running program in at least the following ways:

- As a second daily workout;
- As the easy days in a 6-day-a-week running program;
- As a warmdown after a hard training run;
- As a hard prerace workout;
- To take the place of hill training;
- To roll off the pain and stiffness of a postrace day (it may loosen you up so that you can go out and do another run).

The Bonus that Comes From Indoor Cycling

Increased leg speed and an increased number of turnovers.

Entrainment of breathing to the turnovers. This means that breathing gives a rhythm to the gait and to a change in gait. This is easier to prac-tice on a stationary bicycle than out on the road. In a well-trained athlete, change in breathing comes before the final kick or sprint. Man is the only animal whose breathing rate is not tied to gait turnover on a one-to-one basis because he is the only running biped.

The average runner does between 400 and 600 miles a year. By adding three 30- to 45-minute sessions on an indoor bike every week, you can bring your energy expenditure up to the 2000 calories a week that cardiologists recommend.

Almost no matter what the distance trained, the hazards of running are such that a good general rule is: cut the distance by a third and the chance of injury is halved. Therefore, doubling your mileage from 15 to say 30 miles a week, or—like the running heavies or the truly obsessed—going from 80 to 100 or 120 miles a week, is asking to get hurt. Many coaches say that the second daily workout is the one that really pays off; and if done on an indoor bike it won't increase the chance of injury.

A set of anerobic sprints or hard aerobic intervals once a week can take the place of hill training. This isn't the best way to learn to cycle, but it will build strength in the climbing muscles.

A 2- to 4-minute maximum effort can be used to find the anaerobic threshold; subsequent workouts should be somewhere between 70% and 90% of this point.

Biking Technique

When runners get on bikes they often try to muscle them around at their running pace and do square rather than round pedaling. Articles in triathlon magazines even suggest that this is the way to do it. But the whole art of cycling is making smooth perfect circles with the legs.

Until you get what cyclists call "the feel of the pedal," a lot of your effort is lost. All that bouncing and squirming around does give you a workout, but it also shakes you up. You want to train your leg muscles to fire fast and in that way encourage rapid draining of the blood. That takes smooth pedal action.

It is true that you are not working as hard on a bike as you are running because the bike, instead of your feet, is carrying the weight of your body. Don't try to make up for this by pushing against high resistance; you will just hurt your knees. Instead, try to increase the number of pedal revolutions per minute.

Anyone who is serious about getting the benefits of indoor biking should learn to use toeclips. Toeclips add to your efficiency, make high-level workouts possible and make it easier to feel whether you are pedaling correctly. They also make it possible to exercise with just one leg and thus to preserve fitness while recovering from an otherwise immobilizing injury.

Recovering from Injury

Ernst Van Aaken, the famous German runners' doctor, recommends bicycle training for runners with running injuries. He says, "The basic principle is that stress is taken off the legs, but the circulatory system is kept working.... This has the advantage of continuing to train the endurance functions of heart and circulation.... No other sport is so complementary to running."

Joan Benoit was operated on for a knee injury six weeks before the 1984 Olympics. Her gold medal marathon victory is certainly proof that cycling will get you back in shape for running.

BE A BETTER SKIER

Cross-country skiing is a wonderful aerobic exercise. It is very compatible with bicycling, so if you've been working out on a stationary bicycle you should find yourself being able to enjoy a long day's skiing more than you ever did before.

Downhill skiing, on the other hand, along with tennis, shares the problem of stop-and-go action that stresses the heart without building endurance. Many sudden shifts of position can cause muscle strains and sprains.

"Most holiday skiers do to their bodies for seven days what football players do only once a week," according to Dr. Mitchell Sheinkop, skier and orthopedic surgeon.

Start getting ready at least six weeks before you go—better yet, two months

How do you prevent injury on the slopes? By being in shape when you get there. Work out three days a week, with a rest day in between to give muscles time to rebuild and repair.

For Endurance

The more tired you are, the more likely you are to be injured. On the weekends just before skiing, try to build up to cycling (or any other combination of aerobic sports) *at least* half as long as you plan to ski.

Skiing sometimes calls for very short bursts of hard effort. So, every week or two, you should do one short session of interval training instead of doing a longer aerobic session.

Work up to pedaling 25 minutes on a stationary bicycle. Depending on how fit you are, at the end of a month to six weeks you should be able to do: a 5-minute warmup, then 5 minutes at higher resistance, then with lower resistance do five 60-second sprints with a minute of rest after each, finishing with a 5-minute rolldown.

If you haven't recovered in a minute from the first interval, take as long as you need, pedaling slowly until you are rested. If the second interval is even more tiring, take a very long rolldown and stop. Just knowing that you're not strong enough will make you safer on the slopes because you'll have a better idea of what you can and cannot do.

For Flexibility

Fifteen minutes of stretching exercises should be done after a warmup or rolldown to build flexibility in the hips, lower back and hamstrings. Stretch slowly, hold the position for 20 to 30 seconds after the pain begins; breathe evenly and do not bounce.

Don't turn bicycling into a strength exercise! Use it to build up leg speed and flexibility.

For Strength

Muscle strength in thighs, knees and arms can make the difference between falling and staying upright.

Pushups are for upper-body strength. Start doing pushups from the knee position; when you are stronger, do them from the toes. Work up to three sets of 15.

Do knee bends or single-leg squats to one third down. Hold on to the corner of a table and keep your body upright. Slowly dip the leg to one third down; hold for 30 seconds, slowly bring it back up to standing. To simulate skiing, rotate the knees inward until you feel the weight of your body on the inside of your foot. Work up to doing three sets of 25 of these squats.

On the Slopes

Buy or rent the best equipment you can afford. Make sure the ski bindings will release the boot in a spill.

Take lessons from a professional. Be sure to learn how to get on and off a ski lift, a major source of accidents.

Warm up by doing mild stretching for 5 minutes before each run, as close to the start of the run as possible. (Cold shortens muscles and makes them more prone to injury; stretching lengthens them.)

During the Season

Keep up the indoor biking during the season. You lose half the benefit of the last workout after a week. If you are a weekend skier continue to do two or three midweek sessions of indoor biking to maintain your endurance.

BE A BETTER BIKE RIDER

There's the old joke:
"How do you get to Carnegie Hall?"
"Practice, practice, practice."
There are things you can practice at home on your stationary bicycle that will make bike riding safer and more enjoyable out on the street.

Casual bike riders are afraid to look around and see what's happening in back of them. Looking behind you is the best way to make eye contact with drivers of nearby cars to let them know that you are planning a move and to check that they will allow you enough space to make it.

With the bike on a wind-load simulator you can practice shifting, braking and getting out the water bottle.

Because *any* braking lightens the back wheel, you want to move your center of gravity back to help keep the wheel on the ground. Practice sliding back on the seat when you brake until it's a habit. That will make you less likely to fly over the handlebars after a sudden stop.

Pedaling

The practice of smooth and even pedaling on your stationary bike will make you a better cyclist.

It takes much less time to become a skilled pedaler on a stationary bicycle than on an outdoor bike. There are no distractions. Then, when you take your bike on the road, smooth pedaling will have become a habit. You can judge your capacity for the task and not run out of steam when you muscle up a hill.

There's the "push with both feet" school of pedaling. Many world-class bikers seem to be muscle men, but it's important to get the leg speed first. If you pedal evenly you're not rocking the handlebars constantly; your bike will stay on track. The tedium of all that indoor pedaling should have taught you to hang loose, rather than hanging onto the handlebars for dear life.

Lengthening Rides

Once you can pedal steadily for a half hour, a 20-mile bike ride becomes just as possible as a 5-mile one for a casual biker.

If you've just been a weekend cyclist until now,

you have lost 50% of the benefit of the last ride by the time the next weekend comes around. By using a stationary cycle during the week and on rainy weekends, your endurance will build up to a much higher level.

You'll be able to go for a 35-mile bike ride and still be good for something the next day.

You'll be able to go for as long a bike ride at the beginning of the season as you used to be able to at the end—and, most important, avoid the pain of getting into shape.

You should be able to avoid a lot of overuse injuries.

Equipment

You will have made peace with your bike saddle. (The new leather-covered, foam-padded seats and padded-chamois shorts provide much better insulation than racing saddles.)

10-SPEED HAND POSITIONS. In spite of what you see on TV commercials, you don't *have* to ride the drops on a 10-speed. Even racers ride the top of the bars most of the time.

If you follow our advice and get rattrap pedals, toeclips, toestraps and use a rigid shoe like a bike touring shoe, you'll protect your feet and will ride more safely.

But the mechanical advantage and ease of pedaling with toestraps are secondary to the safety-belt effect once you're out on the road. Toeclips keep you on the bike when a fault in the road might have pitched you off.

Use Your Own Bike

Any indoor cycle should help you become a smoother pedaler, but there are many advantages to using your regular bike for your indoor training. So we recommend either a wind-load simulator or rollers for people who want to really improve their biking.

While you can practice shifting, braking, using toeclips and pedaling when your bicycle is on a stand, rollers can help you practice some things that will make you safer in traffic: sitting up and looking over your shoulder; riding the tops, drops or brake handles with one hand while shifting or signaling with the other.

Minor differences in position make major differences in comfort on long rides. What better place to adjust your bike than at home, where you have the tools at hand?

Try positioning cleats while your bicycle is in the house rather than on the road where a sore knee can make getting home agony. Orthopedists say you shouldn't try to change the way your feet normally face—in, out or straight—when you cycle. It's important not to have the cleats force your feet into an unnatural position.

What old-timers recommend is that you use shoes without cleats for a while and notice the line the pedal makes on the bottom of each sole, then attach the cleat just in front of that line. Often one foot naturally turns in or out more than the other, so this is pretty good advice.

Avoiding Accidents

Your improved health and added skill should make you more alert to traffic. You're also more likely to be able to act in a situation that calls for action—and have the leg power to sprint out of danger.

As good an idea as bike helmets may be, developing good road sense and bike-handling ability is the best insurance against accidents.

Biking Survival Rules

- Keep your bike roadworthy. There's a simple safety check that's easy to do with any bicycle and impossible with most exercise machines: raise the bike about three inches off the ground and slam it down; if anything rattles, find out why and fix it or get it fixed.
- Make sure nothing on you or the carrier can

get caught in the wheels or crank (shoelaces, for example).

- Leave your Walkman at home. Traffic sounds are important clues as to what's happening around you.
- Be alert—you're not in front of the TV. Half of all bicycle accidents involve nothing but a rider, a bike and an immovable object like the curb.
- When sharing the road or a bike path with oncoming runners, it is best to make your move early and show them which side you are going to pass them on.
- Ride with traffic, go with the flow; obey the laws. If you ride against traffic you menace everyone. People do not look for traffic where it's not supposed to be!
- Be predictable. Drivers are, and you're sharing the road with them. Use hand signals and make eye contact whenever possible. If you hide by the curb and ride in the parking zone, then drivers won't know you're there when you pop into their line of vision 20 feet farther on.
- Take as much room as you need, but be prepared to move to the right at any time.
- Be visible. The narrow profile a bike presents to a driver can cause a problem, especially in the rain or dim light.
- Move back on the seat when you brake.
- Wear sneakers or shoes that lace up and have firm soles.

If you're truly afraid of traffic and don't feel up to all of this, *don't do it!* There are already enough fools on the road who shouldn't be out there biking.

Cycling Alternatives to Indoor Cycling

Other machines that use the same pedaling motion that is so good for your heart and so easy on your joints and tendons include tricycles and pedalboats. There is even a mowing machine that lets you cut the grass while cycling. The most popular one, of course, is the bicycle itself. And once you have learned to pedal swiftly and smoothly you have built the endurance that will let you have a wonderful time touring around. In fact, anyone who can stay on an indoor cycle for a half hour has already done more biking than the average 2- to 5-mile ride.

If you have a problem with keeping your balance, a pedalboat or a tricycle might be for you. A friend who was forced off her bike by balance problems and knee injuries found happiness: on land with a two-wheels-in-front tricycle (less tippy); at sea with a pontoon pedalboat that could be entered simply by stepping off the landing, without having to scrunch down, as you do entering most boats.

G

d of fat.

belly. Or hearing about it from friends. Furthermore, weight around your middle is the most likely to cause a heart attack.

Did you know that it is possible to drink beer, watch football all season long, and not gain weight—even to lose weight—if you do a half hour of cycling for every regular beer (20 minutes for a Light)?

This is about the amount of liquid you can and should absorb—12 ounces of liquid for every half hour of pedaling.

You can pedal off a six-pack a game.

The indoor bike is right there, just as near as the refrigerator.

When you go hard, you're burning 400 to 500 calories an hour at about 75% of your aerobic maximum (75% of 220 minus your age). But you have to be in good shape to go this hard for an hour. If you could, you could drink two beers and still have lost from 100 to 200 calories of fat.

At near your aerobic threshold (60%), there should be a pedaling rate that feels just right. You feel you could keep it up for hours.

You can!

This feeling of a good tempo is caused by the breathing and the pedaling finding a rhythm at which everything works well together. If you can keep the pedaling smooth and even, it can be sustained for a very long time.

You're burning 300 to 400 calories an hour (equaling fast walking or bicycling 12+ miles an hour). Keep this up for three hours and you've burned the 900 calories needed to have some aerobic fitness. The beer will replace most of the calories but you will still benefit from the increased endurance that aerobic fitness gives.

If you don't do any other exercise during the week, you lose about half of the aerobic benefits gained by the next weekend. You need only two other workouts of 200 calories to exceed the 1000 calories a week of exercise recommended to get a continuous training effect.

Two 3-hour pedaling sessions/games with two days between them would equal the 2000 calories a week that cardiologists say give maximum heart protection.

So, if you could work in two 45-minute workouts at 75% of your maximum, you'd be in great shape by Superbowl time.

If you don't increase your food intake (beer is food), you should be losing about two pounds a month. Over a winter, instead of gaining eight pounds, you can lose that much.

Bonus Points

Actually, you should lose more weight, because if you're riding a bike you're not snacking. You may even be ready to eat the big Sunday dinner you always have to turn down.

An added advantage of the long indoor biking session is that the afterburner effect continues for a very long time. This should improve your digestion and your sex life as well as controlling the pounds and inches.

If This Sounds Crazy...

Spending 2 hours on an indoor bike may sound dumb, but bike racers train 35 hours a week. Doing it indoors means you don't have to worry about traffic, weather, road rash or dogs.

Thousands of weekend cyclists, many of whom are nowhere near as fit as you are, start the spring season with very modest rides and by September ride 100 or 200 miles a day. The national cyclists' organization, the LAW/Bicycle USA, has been sponsoring September as "The Century Month" (100 miles = 1 century) for as long as we can remember. Local cycling clubs participate, and people earn patches. Lots start just to see if they can do it, then get hooked on it. In any case, it means sitting on a bike for between 5 hours (top riders) and 12 hours (outside limit allowed).

Training Tips for Long Sessions

Pace yourself: warm up thoroughly; save the sprint for the second hour.

Don't muscle the bike around; try to pedal smoothly and evenly.

Always roll down slowly for about 5 minutes before getting off the bike. Rolling slowly drains the pain-producing lactic acid out and allows the muscles to stretch back.

If you get off for more than 5 minutes, you should warm up again. And any time you're planning to get off, do a little rolldown, because you may be interrupted and not get back on.

If you skip a beer, drink a glass of water.

Since you're trying to stay on for a long time, you should consider getting biking clothes. There are a hundred years of practical thinking behind the design of cycling shorts, shoes and gloves, and any or all of these might make the difference between your being able to stay on the bike for 25 minutes and being able to stay on for 1 hour, 2, or even more.

Most pro football and hockey teams use indoor bike training for building endurance. It's almost as hard to hurt yourself on an indoor bike as it is easy to hurt yourself jogging or doing aerobic exercises—or playing football or hockey. It's too easy to get hurt in other ways to risk injury in endurance workouts.

SPECIAL INTERESTS

AGING

Many of the unpleasant physical changes that come with age can be prevented, slowed or even reversed through a program of indoor biking.

Lung Power

This measurement is so important it's called the vital capacity, because your life depends on your getting oxygen from the air. The active person extracts oxygen from the air more efficiently than the inactive one. If you don't exercise, you lose 1% of your lung capacity each year after you're thirty.

That's why it's so important to stay active; and indoor cycling lets you build up your lung power in the safe setting of your home. So it helps reverse some of the natural processes of aging—which often are merely the results of inactivity.

Which means that a seventy-year-old who's been active all his or her life may have a greater vital capacity than a beer-drinking sedentary forty-year-old.

Circulation

The adult heart's ability to get this oxygen to the muscles from the blood declines about 8% every ten years and the arteries narrow as fatty deposits clog them; this increases blood pressure. By middle age, the arterial opening is a third narrower than in a twenty-year-old. Cycling can slow down this process and lower blood pressure; there is even some evidence that the HDL produced sweeps some of the cholesterol from the arteries. And the improved circulation cuts down on edema (no more swollen ankles).

Diabetes Prevention

Besides improving lung function and circulation, exercise increases the number of insulin-binding sites in muscle. This lowers the glucose level in the blood and helps prevent adult-onset diabetes.

Bones and Joints

Bones that are exercised remain strong. So do joints; studies show that there are fewer arthritic changes in active than in sedentary people. If you already have arthritis, cycle gently; you will find there is less stiffness and your range of motion should improve.

Nervous System

Nerve cells also are less likely to age if they are used. And as more oxygen is carried in the blood, more reaches the brain, keeping you alert.

Appetite

The increased vigor increases appetite; many older people get depressed and eat less, which in turn means they often are not getting all the nutrients they need.

Digestion

The improved circulation that comes from indoor cycling also aids digestion and helps prevent constipation, but remember to replace water lost in sweating.

Weight Control

The increased metabolism helps burn off extra fat. It slows the loss of muscle tissue and the conversion of lean body mass into fat. Paul Dudley White, the famous heart doctor, always liked to see his patients over fifty underweight, particularly the muscular barrel-chested types.

Before You Start

Discuss your plans with your doctor and be sure to read "Medical Alert."

Be sure to set reasonable goals; allow yourself six months or a year to get in shape.

All the Benefits

After you've reached maintenance and held it for a year, you've increased your vital capacity by 25%. A fit sixty-year-old has the capacity of the average thirty-five-year-old. Your cholesterol level has dropped, your body has learned to absorb more oxygen, your heart has learned to beat more slowly.

As indoor cycling helps you get stronger, you'll look better, feel better, eat better, sleep better, endure stress better and get more done. You'll lose some of the helpless feeling caused by feeling weak and old.

Important Note

Both warming up and rolling down slowly are particularly important for older people because the circulatory system is less flexible; stopping suddenly is likely to make you feel faint.

If you feel lightheaded or faint, *stay calm:* it is a perfectly normal occurrence; but if you panic, that releases adrenalin which can cause heart rhythm irregularities that can be dangerous.

The older body also adapts less well to heat, so be especially careful to monitor your pulse when it's hot, and always drink enough water to prevent dehydration. Do not wait until you are thirsty, because as you get older you do not feel thirst as strongly but you need water just as much.

WOMEN

Fewer women than men die at an early age of heart attacks because estrogen has a protective effect, at least until menopause. However, more women suffer from brittle bones caused by osteoporosis.

Dr. Dorothy Harris, director of the Center for Women and Sport at Pennsylvania State University, recommends three ways of avoiding osteoporosis: (1) participate in vigorous activity during the growing years to generate strong, dense bones; (2) continue a physically active lifestyle throughout life; (3) include enough calcium in your diet to maintain a proper concentration in the body.

Your Monthly Schedule

Most women are fitter physically during the first half of the menstrual cycle; the lowest point is a few days before menstruation; the highest is immediately after it. But that's only a statistical fact and may not be true for you.

Beryl Burton, for over twenty years one of the world's greatest women cyclists and the only woman who has ever beaten all the men in a national 12-hour time trial, says, "I find the day before my period is due, I can go like a rocket on the bike... but I sure pay for it the next day. I don't suffer with cramps but I feel very lethargic....I feel as though someone has switched me off."

So you, too, are probably going to get "the slows" sometimes and shouldn't expect to do as well during every part of your menstrual cycle. And if you try forcing the same level of effort you may be in for some overtraining symptoms.

Should you cycle during menstruation? Dr. Mona Shangold says, "There is, of course, no reason to avoid athletic participation during menstruation." And notes that both tampons and sanitary napkins are medically acceptable during exercise.

"Many athletes have reported relief of menstrual pain with exercise," she says, and adds that it's not clear why this is true but it seems to be a fact. It could be because of "improved pelvic circulation, increased metabolism of pain-inducing substances, and/or increased production of pain-alleviating substances."

Special Gear

Stationary bikes, like most other bicycles, seem to be designed for men. What does this mean? It assumes a man's anatomy: larger hands, longer arms, wider shoulders, a differently shaped bottom. This means that a bicycle may cause pain because it is not in proportion to your body.

OPEN-FRAME BIKE WITH WIND-LOAD SIMULATOR.
Using a woman's open-frame or unisex mixte-frame bicycle can make getting on
or off much easier than using a man's top-tube model.

Some things to check:

Can you reach the handlebars without straining? If not, you are asking for neck and upper back pain as well as too much pressure on the hands and bottom. On a bicycle, get a shorter stem; on a stationary bike, see if you can tilt the handlebars toward you; see if the saddle can be moved forward without putting your knee in the wrong position.

Are you comfortable on the seat? For how long? You may not find out right away that you have a problem, because a seat may be comfortable for 10 minutes and become an instrument of torture after 30. Read "The Seat" section of "Bike Fit in Detail" extremely carefully; there is enormous variance in pelvic distances, etc. Do not therefore assume, however, that a man's saddle would not be a good fit.

An extra little tip: some machines vibrate, and this can cause numbness and ensuing pain in the clitoral area. Tilting the seat down very slightly, plus cushioning the whole seat, seem to help; try a sanitary napkin, chamois-lined bike shorts and/or a Spenco padded seat cover.

One way of avoiding the problem is having no contact there at all—seats that are just two pads that swivel, no front (an idea first patented around 1880, and reinvented; there are several versions on the market).

Is there too much pressure on your hands? Bike gloves or Spenco pads are helpful.

Urinary Incontinence

Urinary incontinence is a problem for some women, especially after two or three pregnancies. Exercise seems to aggravate it. Indoor biking is a very practical form of aerobic exercise for a person suffering from this. Before you get on the bike, go to the bathroom. Once you've started to sweat and gone aerobic, so much blood is in the muscles and not the inner organs that the urge to urinate lessens.

PREGNANCY

A recent study of pregnant athletes showed that Caesarean births were 50% fewer, labor easier and recovery time shorter than for nonactive mothers.

Since a definition of work is amount of weight moved, you could consider pregnancy a training program by definition since you are getting used to carrying more and more weight.

The American College of Obstetricians and Gynecologists recommended stationary cycling, brisk walking or swimming as the most beneficial types of exercise during pregnancy and after childbirth.

We include here their recommendations for stationary cycling.

What changes in body state affect how much and what kind of cycling to do?

Higher than normal heart rate occurs even at rest; intense exercise results in a greater than usual increase. The response is highly variable and hard to predict, especially in anemic, obese or extremely sedentary women. Monitor your heart rate as you go and do not let it go above 140 beats a minute or 23 beats in 10 seconds. Slow down if you start feeling breathless.

Connective tissues, which include ligaments and tendons, are softened by the hormones produced by pregnancy and remain soft for some months after childbirth. This means they are more vulnerable to injury from stretching or pounding. So roll smoothly, do not pound the pedals.

An increase in maternal body temperature can cause birth defects, and of course exercise does raise the temperature. If the weather is hot or humid so that perspiration can't evaporate, cut down on either rate or time exercising. And use an air conditioner or fan to cool you.

It is easier to get dehydrated during pregnancy, which can interfere with blood circulation and may trigger premature labor. So drink plenty of water before, during and after cycling.

Blood sugar levels are lower, and you burn calories faster, so have a lemon drop or drink diluted fruit juice instead of water if you are feeling a bit faint.

Your need for salt also increases because your fetus requires it. This explains that craving for pickles!

Your center of gravity changes as pregnancy advances, making you more susceptible to falls. Be very careful getting on and off the cycle.

Do Not Exercise Vigorously if You Have:

- A history of miscarriages
- A multiple pregnancy
- Heart disease
- Vaginal bleeding
- A weak cervix
- An abnormally placed placenta (placenta previa)
- Ruptured membranes or premature labor

Medical Conditions That Need Special Approval:

- High blood pressure
- Diabetes
- Obesity
- Thyroid disease
- Kidney disease

CHILDREN AND TEENAGERS

Indoor cycling is particularly helpful to two entirely different types of youngster: the weak, frail child and the overweight one. That's because inactivity is a factor in both conditions.

Indoor cycling builds endurance—and muscles—and also helps the body burn off excess fat. Aerobic exercise increases a thin person's appetite and decreases a fat person's. And this exercise can be done away from the competitive atmosphere and taunts of classmates.

Indoor cycling doesn't have to interfere with homework or quiet recreation, as it is possible to read, study, listen to music or watch TV while exercising.

Fighting Fat

Obesity among children has increased over 50% in the last twenty years. William Dietz of the New England Medical Center Hospitals has studied childhood obesity and is sure that television viewing causes it. "Children eat more when they watch TV and they eat more of the food they see advertised on TV. The message TV conveys is that you'll be thin no matter what you eat."

Sniping at children about their weight is useless. So is imposing a diet without the child's cooperation (or having a fat child offered different food from that of the rest of the family). Both approaches just cause resentment and make a child's obsession with food even stronger.

Overweight children and teenagers are often unhappy. They are the victims of much teasing and self-hate. They want to be thin but don't know how to go about it safely. They often try not to eat at all or to eat just one meal a day, but this makes them logy at school, and then they're so starved when they get home that they stuff themselves. Their attempts to cut down on eating can turn into serious disorders such as anorexia or bulimia.

A pound of fat is 3500 stored calories, so children can become overweight with less than a hundred extra calories a day. Inactivity, not overeating, is to blame in most cases, so children should be encouraged to exercise.

Dietz's early findings show a large drop in metabolism rate when children watch TV—many seem to go into a kind of stupor or trance.

Indoor cycling burns off fat both during and for several hours after the exercise because it raises the metabolism rate.

Fighting Weakness

Thin youngsters who never seem to have enough energy to do anything but lie around and watch TV can be revitalized by a program of indoor cycling. These youngsters are undermuscled for their weight; inactivity has atrophied their muscles. Pushing the pedals pushes air into their lungs and increased strength and appetite come with the increased circulation.

It can be as difficult to get frail youngsters to start exercising as it is to get them to start eating properly. Often they do not feel particularly unhappy. Their parents show that they're concerned about them; and they get out of doing many unpleasant things because they're too weak.

Before You Start Your Child on a Program

Have a medical checkup to make sure it won't harm your child. A phone call to the pediatrician may be enough to get clearance.

If your child has asthma, diabetes, heart disease or some other disabling condition, exercise may still be good for him or her, especially if it's monitored by you at home. Discuss this possibility with the doctor.

It is leg length, not height, that determines whether a child can fit on a bike or not. Most 10- or 12-year-olds will fit on some—not all—exercise bikes. Look for ones that have more upright seat posts. Pedal blocks for children's bicycles can be put on, and a thinner seat can make up for an extra inch or two.

Set up the bike carefully, according to the directions in the "Bike Fit" section. Check every month or so to make sure the seat is still high enough and the handlebars allow for easy breathing. Have the child wear firm-soled shoes or sneakers—the same ones each time, as sole thickness affects seat height.

Children too small to fit on an indoor cycle should be encouraged to dance, run and play, ride a tricycle or stand and talk to you while you pedal. You should be so energized by your exercise that you'll have more untired time to accompany them on walks or play tag or badminton with them.

Set a time and a place for your child to cycle: during cartoons or a favorite show, or after dinner on Monday, Wednesday, and Friday. If your child is very unfit, start with 5 minutes: 1 minute at no pressure to warm up, then slowly increase the pressure and ride with increased pressure for 3 minutes (not pushing too hard), then lower the pressure and ride for 1 minute to cool off before stopping.

Work up by an extra minute each time until at the end of ten weeks the child's doing maintenance—3 to 5 minutes warmup and cooldown, 20 minutes in between.

Set an example. Get a stationary bicycle and be too busy and happy to talk to the child until you've finished your workout. Talk it up! Show

how having more energy makes you happy. Note that riding a regular bike will be easier and that you'll be able to enjoy longer rides. Mention that coaches of professional baseball, football and hockey teams all have their players use indoor cycles to build endurance.

Get two stationary bicycles and make a game of seeing who can pedal the most miles while reading or watching TV. Pin up a map and see if you can go across the state.

If you don't need the extra exercise or the above doesn't work, play the heavy parent and say no watching TV, reading books or sitting around daydreaming (or whatever keeps the kids from exercising) unless they cycle first.

Everything we advise about how to start, pedal and set reasonable goals is just as important for children and adolescents as it is for adults. So is drinking enough water to replace the amount that was lost during exercise. And, since results are not immediate but take a month or so to be seen and felt, encouragement to continue is necessary at first.

On the other hand, once children start feeling better, you may have to monitor them to make sure they aren't overdoing it.

CONDITIONS CYCLING HELPS

BACKACHES

Continuing back pain plagues 31 million Americans and is the most frequent cause of lost work time in people under forty-five. Indoor cycling helps prevent backache in three ways: by lessening stress, by stretching the vertebrae and by fighting obesity. However, to avoid damage to the spinal column, it is also necessary to have strong trunk muscles in order to lift and carry heavy objects correctly.

Thousands have benefited from back courses in which physical therapists teach people the mechanics of bending, lifting and carrying things properly—and how to stretch and strengthen the back, stomach and large-extremity muscles. If you do have a back problem, it is particularly important to have a qualified person teach you how to exercise. Too many untrained trainers take pride in how hard they work their exercise classes—avoiding such teachers is probably the only time not exercising is better for your health.

Many overweight people have backaches—especially those who have added a lot of weight to their abdomens. It's logical. This weight throws you off balance, putting additional strain on muscles and spine. Indoor cycling lets you exercise some of that weight away without straining your back.

A lot of backaches come on very suddenly.

Glenn Goldfinger, project coordinator of the New York Regional Spinal Cord Injury System at the New York University Medical Center for Rehabilitative Medicine, describes the sudden onset of the typical crippler:

"A sneeze, cough, reach or move that is well within one's normal movement repertoire suddenly brings on pain. Physical therapists who specialize in musculo-skeletal disorders can relieve this pain, but after the acute phase, a long-term exercise program should also be initiated to reduce the tension levels in the body."

Goldfinger points to the real cause: "The coupling of ever-increasing tensions and diminishing physical exercise produce abnormal levels of muscular tension in the body, which, when combined with slight physical activity, yield strains, sprains, and a condition called tension myositis....

"Because tension myositis usually strikes the neck, shoulder and low-back regions, care must be taken to select the best form of aerobic exercise.

"Bicycle riding, specifically stationary bicycle riding, is probably the safest, most consistent, nonweather-dependent and cheapest form of intense aerobic exercise existing today.

"The stationary bicycle, whether at home or in a health club, is accessible 365 days a year. The body will not be jarred while riding it, and one can breathe relatively clean indoor air as opposed to exhaust fumes from a street."

STRESS

Anything that a person perceives as a threat causes a stress reaction. The body secretes hormones to mobilize its energy resources for fight or flight. Adrenalin floods your system, your heart beats faster.

The body doesn't differentiate between physical and mental threats. It reacts the same way whether you're faced by a lion or a job interview.

Since you might bleed, in a fight, stress makes the blood clot faster. Anyone with blockage of the blood vessels is put in danger: blood clots can be fatal.

In a well-conditioned body the blood takes longer to clot because exercise causes lysing. Lysing is the breakdown of minute clots in the blood. It happens when an enzyme in the blood locates clots and dissolves them.

On the other hand, some kinds of exercise are stressful. Unfamiliar, exhausting or competitive exercise have all been shown to accelerate clotting time.

What this means to the person choosing indoor cycling to build aerobic endurance is this: the first time you get on a stationary bicycle, take it easy, especially if you have never ridden a regular bicycle. Don't go so long or so fast that you feel you could drop. Let your body—not the dials or some program you're trying to follow—tell you how hard to push.

Signs of Stress

Some physical signals that show the body's habitual response to stress is becoming destructive:
- Feeling breathless
- Cold hands, especially if one is colder than the other
- Aching jaws, often caused by clenching teeth
- Muscle spasms or tightness in the back of the neck, shoulders or lower back
- Frequent urination
- Indigestion, diarrhea
- Headaches
- Tiredness, insomnia or sleeping too much
- Becoming suddenly accident-prone
- Catching every cold or virus that's going around (Chronic stress weakens the immune system.)

In one study that showed exercise helps you cope better with stress, blood pressure, muscle tension and anxiety levels were measured in two groups both before and after one of them participated in a 14-week exercise program at the Human Performance Laboratory in San Francisco. As might be expected, the exercising group scored lower in all three measures afterward, and the other did not.

To see how they reacted to stress, the students were then given a test consisting of mostly insoluble problems and were told that it was a good indicator of how they were likely to perform in college. Both groups were told they did poorly on the test. The aerobic-conditioned group showed less increased muscle tension and anxiety; and, most important, *no* increase in blood pressure—proof that aerobic conditioning had helped it handle stress better.

Dr. Kenneth Greenspan of the Center for Stress Related Disorders suggests that an increase in self-confidence leads to an increase in your sense of control over your life and eliminates chronic stress. If you love what you're doing at work and know how and when to ease up, you won't feel "bad" stress.

If you feel in control of your life, you can channel the stressful energy that goes with the drive to succeed and actually become healthier. The ability to control stress is within every one of us. Bad stress is not triggered by decision making but by feeling powerless.

Many people have turned to exercise to control stress because it is one area that is within our control. You decide when, where, how and how long to do it.

HYPERTENSION

By now we hope that all our readers have had their blood pressure checked—preferably several times over the period of a month—*by a doctor or a nurse. You can't tell whether you have high blood pressure in any other way. (That's why it's called "The Silent Killer.")*

Average Blood Pressure = 120 over 80; Borderline = 140 over 90.

If you have *no* blood pressure, you're dead: it's created as the heart pumps blood through the arteries and meets resistance from their walls. It is highest during a heartbeat (the first number measured) and lowest between beats (the second number). It goes up when the arteries squeeze the blood, and when the amount of blood pushed by the heart increases (like during exercise)—which is the whole idea behind stress tests.

Warmups: a small steady increase can be taken by your inner tubing—your veins and arteries; sudden surges can cause the walls to blow, just like any rubber. Aging makes blood vessels less flexible (that's what the bypasses are all about, and why the older you are the more slowly you should warm up and the more thoroughly you should cool down). You should also avoid sprinting—suddenly going faster—or trying to get the dial to reach 40mph.

Many mechanisms are involved in high blood pressure. On the mechanical level, the arteries and veins are narrower. This could be inherent or caused by a spasm or pinching at some point. Part of this mechanism is the same that makes water fountains such fun for kids. Narrow the opening with your finger and the stream of water can even drench the ceiling because the pressure has been so much heightened.

Risks of High Blood Pressure

Even a small increase in hypertension adds to the risk of stroke, heart attack, kidney damage, blindness. Combined with high cholesterol and smoking, the risk of a heart attack is twelve times greater.

Stress and Hypertension

Dr. Robert S. Eliot, cardiologist and director of the National Center for Preventive and Stress Medicine in Phoenix, has for the last ten years been monitoring how people react to simulated stresses, such as mental arithmetic or video games programmed to make winning harder and harder.

He has concluded that there are some people —about one in five—who may seem cool on the outside, but are "hot reactors"; adrenalin floods their systems and their blood pressure skyrockets —even over 200—whenever they are stressed. And some heat up thirty or forty times a day. "The heart seems to be able to withstand steady high pressures," Eliot says, "but it can't handle surges. It's like drag-racing with the family car. With years of that kind of treatment, the standard engine wears out."

Eliot advises doctors to simulate stress during blood pressure checkups: take it once while resting, give you a tough problem (or yell at you) and take it again.

"Stress may be the greatest single contributor to illness in the industrialized world," says Eliot, who had a stress-induced heart attack eleven years ago, "but I've discovered two rules to live by: Rule No. 1 is don't sweat the small stuff. Rule No. 2 is that it's all small stuff."

Get an Accurate Reading

James Lynch, director of the Psychophysiological Clinic of the University of Maryland Medical School, says that talking (especially to a doctor), climbing stairs or smoking just before a test can raise pressure 10% to 50%.

Lynch encourages his patients to check their blood pressure at home and on the job to find out what events trigger high readings. "Frequently the person who thinks his blood pressure is up has low blood pressure, and vice versa. That's why self-monitoring is absolutely necessary."

Awareness itself can help cool down reactions to stress. A Seattle study showed that 43% of hypertensives were able to lower their blood pressure 10 mm Hg or more after only a month of self-monitoring.

How Cycling Helps Control Hypertension

High blood pressure can be lowered by the improvement in circulation and lessening of edema brought about by using what Dr. Mondenard calls "the good medicine"—aerobic training on an indoor bicycle....

One third of all overweight people have high blood pressure; another reason biking is such good medicine is that fat is burned off; very often blood pressure is lowered when people lose weight.

With exercise, compounds called lysines are released; they decrease the clotting time of blood, making stroke less likely to happen. And as exercise increases the metabolism rate, the white cells have a chance to scavenge out dying blood corpuscles—this short-circuits the process that produces arterosclerosis.

"One of the benefits of exercise is that it breaks down the hypertonic or increased tone as it dilates the vessels of the skin and the vessels to and in the muscles. Local tissue chemical responses do this —it is not something that is centrally mediated,"

Dr. Samuel Fox, director of the Cardiology Exercise Program at Georgetown University Hospital, explains in *The Bicycling Book*.

He adds, "My personal recommendation for the hypertensive patient is to get out and get exercise producing a sweat every day. Keep it up thereafter for at least ten minutes."

How to Cycle if You're Hypertensive

Warm up slowly and thoroughly, and also do a thorough rolldown each time. Keep the resistance fairly low; instead, work on improving the number of your pedal revolutions per minute. Do a workout—even if only 10 or 15 minutes long—every day, twice a day if possible.

Avoid gripping the handlebars tightly; this is a form of isometric exercise—you're contracting a muscle but not moving anything else. When you do that, it causes a sudden increase in blood pressure. You should also avoid lifting, pushing or pulling heavy objects, such as putting spare tires on cars.

Drugs and/or Exercise

If you have mild high blood pressure, your doctor has probably already told you that you have the choice of changing your life-style or having to take drugs.

Endurance training can help you reduce the dosage and stabilize your need for them.

Experiments matching drug therapy and aerobic training show that in the beginning the drugs control the condition faster; but after about five months of exercising, the aerobic groups showed greater improvement than the drug-taking group.

However, you shouldn't interpret anything you read in our book as an excuse not to take your medicine. When you tell your doctor that you want to start exercising, he'll probably be happy you're finally following his advice.

Calcium and Hypertension

Dietary studies have shown that hypertensives seem to consume much less calcium—at least 20% less than the rest of the population.

There seem to be at least two kinds of hypertensives. If your blood pressure goes up when you add salt and you have mild hypertension, you are probably one of those who can be helped by calcium supplements (approximately a third of all hypertensives); these people can be identified by a low level of the kidney hormone renin in the blood. High-renin hypertensives, who usually have severe hypertension, should not have calcium supplements.

Perhaps you should discuss the possibility of calcium supplements with your doctor; spontaneously hypertensive rats had their blood pressure virtually normalize when calcium was added to their diet.

HEART

Dr. Paul Dudley White's 8 Coronary Risk Factors:

1. Heredity: other people in immediate family who died of heart disease at a young age
2. Body build: "mesomorph"—barrel-chested, muscular, sloping shoulders, heavy across middle of body
3. Diabetes or gout
4. Smoking cigarettes
5. High blood pressure
6. Gross overweight
7. Excess cholesterol
8. Inactivity—a sedentary life style

The American Heart Association added three in their 1980 list:

1. Stress, personality behavior patterns
2. Abnormal resting EKG
3. Oral contraceptives

The first two on Dr. White's list are determined by heredity, and the tendency to diabetes and gout is also partly inherited, but the other five are more or less under our control.

Indoor bicycling helps eliminate three, as it makes you more active and helps get rid of excess weight and cholesterol.

It is the exercise of choice of cardiac rehabilitation clinics throughout the country, since you

113

can get fit without strain if you set and follow reasonable goals.

Exercise increases the number of high-density lipoproteins in the blood, which lowers the TOTAL-HDL ratio that is considered the most important determinant of coronary risk by Dr. William P. Castelli, director of the Framingham Heart Study.

Dr. Castelli studied some cyclists and found that 2 hours of cycling a week was enough to achieve a low TOTAL-HDL ratio. Frequent moderate exercise to maintain a constant flow of HDL cholesterol is better than a long session only once a week.

Of course diet makes a difference too. Our "What to Eat" chapter explains the whole cholesterol question thoroughly and lists what foods help decrease it.

Dr. Paul Dudley White, the cardiologist who just about started the coronary risk lists and who treated President Eisenhower among others, advised James Michener following the author's heart attack, to give up dairy fats and eggs, to walk away from tense situations, to exercise vigorously —but also to take a nap each day.

Take It Easy on Your Heart

If you are at risk of heart disease and are not exercising under medical supervision, be especially careful to warm up and roll down gradually; when the heart has to change its rate too quickly, this puts strain on the whole circulatory system. Ideally the rolldown should be just as long as the warmup. This takes great self-control, but you will feel better for having cooled down while still on the cycle; the sweat will disappear gradually, and you will not be tempted to plunge into a shower or bath to wash it off—another shock to the cardiovascular system you should avoid. Allow at least 10 minutes after you have stopped sweating before showering.

If you have heart disease, avoid isometric exercises, like pushing heavy weights, or the stretch that has you pushing the wall down. These cause a surge in blood pressure and can trigger cardiac irregularities. Also avoid gripping the handlebars tightly—hold them firmly but loosely.

Another Risk Factor

Men with potbellies have a four times higher rate of strokes or heart attacks than those with comparable amounts of weight on their hips. Similarly, women with the highest waist-to-hip ratio had eight times as many heart attacks as those with the lowest ratios.

Heart attacks and strokes are usually caused by blockage of arteries or veins. Since most of the vital organs are in the trunk of the body, the circulation is best there. Therefore abdominal fat gets into the bloodstream more readily than hip fat.

The more fat that circulates in the blood, the greater the chance of developing clogged arteries.

Every time you put on weight you're adding fat to the bloodstream; this explains why losing weight and then gaining it back is more dangerous than staying slightly overweight.

The good news for you if you have this build is that fat builds up in your belly region first and it should go quickly when you're burning more calories than you're taking in.

Women and Heart Disease

While heart attacks are less common for women, they are deadlier: death rate is 25% higher in the first thirty days after an attack, and continues higher for six years.

Women are more than twice as likely to suffer a second heart attack within six years (40% for women, 17% for men).

Female sex hormones protect against heart disease: the heart attack rate increases fourfold after menopause, and also goes up after surgical removal of the ovaries. If you are at risk, you might discuss estrogen replacement therapy with your physician; it also helps prevent osteoporosis.

Heart Attack During Exercise

Chances are greatest during violent exercise—if you're not used to it. The more you exercise regularly, the less likely you are to suffer cardiac arrest during exercise.

The Oregon Health Sciences University did a ten-year study of 40 sports facilities run by the Oregon YMCA that showed only one cardiac arrest and one fatal attack in 2 million man hours of exercise—making it a million-to-one shot.

ARTHRITIS

Arthritis has been with man since caveman days; many doctors consider it an unpleasant but normal accompaniment to middle age. There does seem to be more injury-caused arthritis in young people.

Orthopedic Injury Often Results in Arthritis

Debilitating arthritis often develops after orthopedic injuries. Dr. David Sikes, a rheumatologist and semiprofessional racing car driver from Tampa, Florida, treats young, retired professional athletes who have severe arthritis as a result of injuries.

"You can fix the bones," he says, "but not the cartilage and soft tissue."

115

One more reason to have exercise be easy on joints and soft tissues (like indoor cycling).

Arthritis More Likely to Develop in the Overweight

Excess weight puts stress on aging joints. And if you do have arthritis in your weight-bearing joints, losing weight will make you feel less pain. If you combine indoor cycling with a reasonable diet, you should be able to burn off fat and gain mobility, as long as you don't overdo it.

Exercise and Arthritis

Doctors never recommend exercise during inflammation and suggest you consult your physician before starting any exercise program. But most doctors want you to exercise to maintain function and keep limber. Unfortunately, the pain of moving at all tends to discourage arthritics from exercising.

But you can limit your movement right into a wheelchair if you give in without a fight.

That doesn't mean you should torture yourself.

Warm up slowly and do a sensible buildup without too much resistance. You'll find that pain will diminish greatly and mobility will increase from a program of regular exercise.

If even this much is too much, there are special courses of exercises for arthritics in swimming pools; the buoyancy makes movement easier.

Keep Warm

Cold is a big enemy. It shortens muscles and makes joints ache. Some arthritics find that a hot shower (easier to get in and out of than a bath) is necessary for warming up.

We recommend easy stretches under the warm water...the indoor bike could be right there in the bathroom (use a can of spray lubricant to protect it from the moisture). If not, dress in a sweat suit to conserve the heat and get on the machine while you are still relaxed from the damp heat.

Hand Exercises

The following hand exercises are recommended by the Orthopaedic Institute of the Hospital for Joint Diseases in New York City (the nation's largest voluntary nonprofit orthopedic and rheumatologic hospital and research facility).

Do them ten times each, twice a day.

1. The palms of the hands should be turned toward the floor, then up to the ceiling.
2. Make a fist, then open the fingers and the thumb.
3. Make a circle with both wrists. Then reverse the direction.
4. Touch the end of your thumb to each fingertip in succession, opening your hand after each one.
5. With your hand open, spread your fingers. Then close them gently.

6. Beginning with fingertips pressed together, flatten hands to a prayer position with fingers spread apart. Then reverse the process with mild resistance.

OSTEOPOROSIS

In order for bones to stay strong, they have to be weight-bearing, which is why swimming, while very good for your cardiovascular health, really doesn't help prevent osteoporosis. The exercise doesn't have to be very strenuous, however.

Dr. Everett Smith, head of the Biogerontology Lab at the University of Wisconsin, had a group of women whose average age was eighty-four, perform a gentle exercise program of toe taps, arm lifts, sideward bends and slow knee lifts three times a week for 30 minutes. The exercise not only stopped the loss of bone minerals but also stimulated the bones to produce new cells, thus maintaining or increasing bone mass.

According to Dr. Smith, the mechanical stress on bones stimulates the growth of bone cells called osteoblasts. The increase in bone formation, he says, is directly proportional to the amount of stress applied.

Other studies have shown 20% more bone-mineral content in the legs of middle-aged runners than in those of inactive people the same age, and a loss of up to 39% of bone mass when men were confined to bed for thirty-six weeks.

Stationary cycling is particularly good for preventing osteoporosis because you can do it for so long without much strain. If you are particularly at risk according to the risk factors listed below, you might want to alternate (not combine!) the cycling with some upper arm stretches and some light weight lifting. We do mean light! Take a 16-ounce can of vegetables in each hand (or a pound weight, whichever you prefer), lift it to the shoulder, then over the head and back. Work up to doing this twenty times every other day. If that's too heavy, start with an 8-ounce can.

What Is Osteoporosis?

A disease causing bones to become brittle and thin from loss of bone mass. It affects between 15 and 20 million people in the United States. Every year 1.3 million fractures attributable to osteoporosis occur in people age forty-five and over. Hips break, leaving the patient unable to walk; spinal vertebrae collapse, causing a "crush fracture" with the agony of bones pressing on nerves.

A 1984 National Institutes of Health (NIH) consensus conference called osteoporosis a major

117

public health problem that may be reduced in incidence by exercise and increased calcium intake in earlier life.

Who's at Risk?

Everyone. At greater risk:
- Women more than men.
- Whites and orientals more than blacks.
- Elderly more than young (age slows calcium absorption).
- Underweight or light bone structure, including anorexics.
- It runs in the family (hereditarily prone).
- Postmenopausal, especially surgically induced (estrogen protects bone). The NIH conference concluded that "estrogen replacement therapy is highly effective for preventing osteoporosis in women."
- Sedentary (NIH recommended weight-bearing exercise to prevent bone loss).
- Women who are obsessive exercisers, who may exercise to point of estrogen deficit from fat loss.
- Alcoholics, heavy smokers.

Are You Getting Enough Calcium?

68% of the United States population doesn't get enough calcium.

80% of all women, including 87% of females between the ages of fifteen and eighteen, and 84% of females between the ages of thirty-five and fifty do not get enough calcium.

How Much Calcium Do You Need Daily?

NIH recommended 1000 mg for adults, 1200 mg for teenagers, 1500 mg for pregnant, lactating or postmenopausal women not on estrogen replacement therapy.

What Is 1000 MG?

Each of the following contains 1000 mg of calcium: 3½ glasses of skim milk; 7 ounces of sardines with bones; 5 ounces of hard cheese; 3½ ounces of Swiss cheese; 27½ ounces of Tofu (soybean curd); 5 cups of cooked farina; about 6 cups of cooked spinach or broccoli; 10 cups of cooked navy, lima or kidney beans.

Should You Take Supplements or Food?

As much calcium as possible should be part of your diet, supplemented by the rest. If you are one of the 50 million lactose intolerant adults in the United States today, or have to watch your cholesterol level closely, it is almost impossible to get enough calcium without taking supplements.

What Supplement Should You Take?

Calcium carbonate contains the most elemental calcium—40%. A cheap source can be antacids like Tums and Alka-2, but they contain aluminum, which is bad for your bones. A small amount of vitamin D should also be included in the diet or as a supplement because it is necessary for calcium to be absorbed properly, but more than 2000 IUs a day are not safe, since vitamin D builds up in the body. Dolomite or bone meal may contain lead.

When Should You Take It?

Before bedtime may be best. By then you know about how much dietary calcium you've gotten. Acid is needed for absorption, and at night there's acid in your stomach. This may also protect against bone mass loss during the night. On the other hand, you often have to take six pills or more to get what you need, so some spacing is advised. Large amounts of calcium at mealtimes may impair zinc and iron absorption, but you may have to take it with meals to avoid stomach upset.

119

MEDICAL PROBLEMS

ACHES AND PAINS

Aches and pains have three main causes: a bad fit between the bike and the rider, poor pedaling technique or trying to do too much too fast.

Seat position and comfort are crucial. Too high, too low, too far forward, too far back—all can cause injury. And if your seat is not comfortable or level, you may sit on it lopsided, which can cause knee, hip and back pain because it effectively makes one leg longer than the other. (But check that it isn't the seat which is lopsided.)

Any disparity in fit between you and the bike will be aggravated by longer or more difficult workouts. When you go beyond your conditioning level, you are asking for overuse injuries.

Duration, intensity, frequency—the three measures of working out—must be increased gradually. Injuries happen most often when you try to move to a new level of training too quickly.

The most serious injuries are caused by increasing the intensity: how hard you work. If you increase the resistance too much or too quickly, or start sprinting or doing intervals—especially without first warming up thoroughly—you can easily tear something.

If you suddenly double the length of a workout, or try to make up for lost time the day before by adding to it the next day, you'll feel stiff and sore for a day and no big harm done. But if you suddenly make such a big jump in duration and do it regularly without working up to it, you are asking for big trouble.

How frequently you work out should also be changed gradually. One reason for the day-on, day-off or alternating hard and easy days schedules is to give the muscles, joints and tendons time to recover from the small strains and to repair the small tears caused by the workout.

First Aid

First aid for most muscle, tendon and joint pains:

Stop riding. Rest that part of the body.

Put ice on it. This numbs the pain and keeps swelling down. Since you're at home, you can grab something from the freezer and put it on the sore spot immediately; frozen bread, for example, makes a handy ice pack.

Wrap it up. Bind it up with something firm but stretchy like an Ace bandage. This keeps the blood from rushing to the injury and helps prevent later swelling. The technical term is "compression."

Raise it up. Prop it up on a pillow, lift it. Again, the idea is to keep blood from pooling in that area. The technical term is "elevation."

Orthopedists and gym teachers have an acronym for first aid treatment: RICE. This stands for

Rest, Ice, Compression, and Elevation.

Call a doctor if you think you've torn something or the pain is really intense in spite of the first aid.

Later treatment. Heat and massage help. Aspirin reduces swelling but is hard on the stomach lining, so take it after you've eaten something.

After two days, apply ice before you cycle again and do a very easy short workout. Apply ice afterward as well. Call a doctor if the pain is severe or if it still hurts three or four days later, or if you have trouble moving it. Be sure to explain what exercise you've been doing. It helps if you go to a sports medicine doctor; other doctors may tell you to stop riding even when it's not necessary, rather than suggesting how to keep the injury from happening again.

Knee Pain

This is never something to be ignored, because the knee can take months to recover from injury and can be permanently damaged if you persist in riding with pain.

As soon as you feel pain, lower the gear or the resistance. Knee pain is often caused by pushing against too much resistance, raising the resistance without enough warmup or trying to increase the length of the workout too quickly. If the knee still hurts, roll down, then stop pedaling. Give it at least a day's rest, or more if it hurts when you're

walking. Strength training helps prevent a recurrence of pain caused by overtraining or too much resistance.

Incorrect seat or foot position can cause knee pain. Pain on the outside of the knees can be caused by a seat that's too far forward or too low. Make sure your seat hasn't slipped down. Pain under the kneecap is often caused by too high a seat. The angle of the foot on the pedal should be the same as that foot's normal walking angle or an unnatural strain is placed on the knee. All this is explained fully in "Bike Fit." Your ankle rolling inward too much (pronation) can also cause knee trouble; the cure is an arch support.

If pain occurs while you're pedaling and you don't want to stop, look down and see if your foot is at a strange angle. Try changing the angle a little and see if the pain stops after a minute or two. If it still doesn't go away, get off the bike and reassess the fit completely. Have you changed your shoes? Riding with a sole that is thicker or thinner is the equivalent of raising or lowering the seat.

Hand Pain and/or Numbness

Too much pressure on the hands can damage the ulnar nerve in the wrist and make your hands feel numb all the time. Padding the handlebars and the hands can help. A good bike store has handlebar padding, padded tape for bars the molded-to-fit padding doesn't fit, padded gloves and palm pads.

People with short arms may have to lean too far forward to reach the handlebars, which puts too much of the weight of the body on the hands. Try raising the handlebars and tilting them toward you. If that doesn't help, you may need a shorter stem. Don't push the seat nearer without making sure the knee isn't in front of the pedal axle, or you may trade hand pain for knee pain.

Seat Pain

Sometimes the seat feels fine the first day but hurts on the second or third. It feels as if you've bruised yourself—and you have. A seat feels comfortable if it supports you in the right place and if you've gotten used to it and built some "seat calluses."

This kind of seat pain can be expected just after starting training or if you're returning to it after a long layoff. Often this pain goes away after five minutes of cycling. Check to see if your hips sway as you pedal; try to correct this. Sliding back on the seat a little sometimes helps.

If your seat bones still hurt, you probably need a different saddle or more padding.

Saddle Sores

Saddle sores are caused by friction and bacteria, which love a hot, sweaty environment. Absolute cleanliness helps; Balneal, a cream, both sanitizes and soothes. Bike racers, who may be on a bike for seven hours at a stretch, recommend washing shorts and underwear with a mild soap rather than detergent. They may also use Balneal, A & D ointment or a powder to prevent chafing.

Hemorrhoids

A more upright position, padded anatomic touring seat with a small indentation between the cheekbone pads at the back, and/or Lycra bike shorts with padded chamois are all worth trying.

Penile Numbness

Penile numbness can be caused by friction from loose clothing or having the seat too low, too thickly padded, tilted upward too much, or not back far enough. Check seat position and wear underwear and shorts that fit tightly enough to give support—or an athletic supporter (the original jock strap is a Bike brand).

Vaginal Irritation or Numbness

Make sure the seat is absolutely level. On a 10-speed, make sure the seat is no higher than the handlebars; the same level or lower is more comfortable for most women.

Women may have to go the sling-saddle "no seat" way, but bikes aren't really built to be ridden with this saddle, so first try a position that lets you sit almost straight up. Then try Spenco's seat pad and/or padded shorts and an anatomical saddle with the front level or even down a bit. Too much padding may also cause irritation.

Foot Pain

Foot pain can be prevented and often be cured by using stiff-soled cycling shoes that distribute the pressure on the pedal over the whole foot. A foam insole cushions the foot and further lessens the pressure. If the toes hurt, perhaps the toeclips or the shoes are too short.

Neck or Upper Back Pain

The neck is not used to the weight of the head when leaning forward. Ride sitting a little straighter, get used to it a little at a time. If it continues, it may be a sign of cervical arthritis, common in people over forty. This condition is aggravated by sitting forward.

Shoulder, Arm or Elbow Pain

A narrow handlebar or scrunched up position can cause this.

Hip Pain

This is rare in cyclists; often people who can't walk because of hip pain can cycle. If it does occur, it is probably caused by overtraining, or a difference in crank length, or something wrong with the way the bike is set up.

Ice the sore area immediately after cycling, later apply a heating pad. Rest for at least two days. Stretch after riding. Ride at a lower resistance and for less time. If the hip still hurts, you will have to stop cycling—perhaps for as long as a month.

Lower Leg Pain

Overdoing it, working beyond your conditioning level or too much ankling (moving the ankle around while you pedal, instead of keeping the foot fairly level) can cause tibial or Achilles tendonitis. These require rest, ice, and no movement for twenty-four to forty-eight hours; then heat. If they still hurt, see a doctor.

Muscle Cramps

Find the belly of the muscle and press down hard with your thumb, then slowly try to take the leg through its range of motion. If you press the wrong spot, it won't do any harm. Try again. Later on, take an aspirin and massage gently.

If you get cramps often after riding, you may need arch supports—or you may need to replace minerals lost in sweat. Bananas, oranges, pretzels, calcium tablets or a dilute version of Gatorade are traditional bike cures. Some people find that cramps can be avoided if they don't bend their knees up above their hips when they lie down.

Sore Muscles

Beginners at almost any sport have sore muscles as part of the conditioning process, especially if they're pushing themselves too hard. But this soreness should go away in a day or so.

If your leg muscles are sore while you're riding, you either haven't warmed up enough or you are going at it too hard. At the anerobic level the muscles are starved for oxygen, and lactic acid builds up. This process causes pain. One reason we recommend a rolldown (pedaling at a lower rate and with less resistance) is that it washes the lactic acid out of the muscles.

Some people find stretching helpful after a workout; massaging your leg (always toward the heart) also helps get the kinks out.

Delayed Muscle Pain

Some overuse pains take a day or two to appear, so you might not realize they're caused by the exercise. If you're stiff in the morning, have trouble walking down the stairs or operating a clutch pedal, you have probably been overdoing either the intensity, duration or speed of your cycling. Don't ignore the pain and try to do your usual workout. On the other hand, a short session at a low resistance will improve the circulation and remove the lactic acid or the water that is pressing against the pain receptors.

OVERTRAINING

What they never tell you about exercise bikes is just how easy it is to overdo it on one!

That really good workout with three or four hard sprints to see if you can get the dial to read 25mph for a few seconds can leave you weary and shaken for a couple of days. If you had jogged half as far, you would have slowed down to a walk before you cooked yourself and you'd have known enough not to make a second or third hard push.

Depression, unwarranted pessimism, loss of interest in life, loss of appetite, constant tiredness, trouble sleeping, achy joints, general soreness and "the slows" can all be signs of overtraining.

All that is bad enough, but overtraining cuts your resistance to infection. Small cuts don't heal, and you seem to go from one cold to another. Being tired all the time can slow your reflexes; you can become accident prone.

Who Is at Risk?

Overtraining is always a danger with athletes, who often try to push themselves to the limit and tend to think that the only cure for bad performance is to work harder. Often a coach or trainer has to tell them when to lay off. Otherwise they may not recognize that they're going stale because they're training too hard.

People who are trying to gain endurance can make the same mistakes. It's sometimes hard to judge when you're overloading the system enough to build strength and when you're overloading it until it starts to break down.

The time of greatest danger of overtraining is when you are trying to get to a new level of fitness. Sudden or large increases in any of the three measures of training can bring it on.

Exercising too hard may not be the only culprit in your suffering from the overtraining syndrome. Life stresses, whether at home, at work or at school, can combine with your regular workout to push you over the edge. So can losing too much weight or losing weight too quickly.

When extending the length of the aerobic part of your workout, increasing your rolldown will help prevent overtraining.

Are You Overtraining?

You should always feel better after you exercise once your heart has returned to its resting state. If you are still tired, rest thoroughly and eat many small meals.

Check yourself in the morning to see how you do on the following indexes to overtraining.

Overtraining Measures

Pulse index. Before getting up, take the pulse for 60 seconds. Average the daily rates for a week. When the morning pulse is five or more beats above normal, suspect overtraining or illness. Take a day off.

Weight index. Take your weight each day after you use the toilet but before breakfast. Average the daily weights for a week. Rapid or continued weight loss could indicate overtraining, dehydration, illness or not eating enough to balance your calorie expenditure.

Temperature index. Take your temperature each morning for a week; average it. If your temperature is up, you may have an infection. Take a day off.

Fatigue index. How do you feel when you get up?

1. Peppy, raring to go
2. Fresh and rested
3. Pretty good
4. Okay—nothing special
5. Slightly tired
6. Very tired
7. Ready to drop

Levels 4 through 7 all mean you should review what you've been doing. "The social ramble ain't restful," as Satchel Paige said.

Have you been drinking enough water? Be

careful not to overdo if you reach Level 5. Just do a slow warmup at Level 6.

If you're really exhausted (Level 7), check your temperature and what your urine looks like (if it's dark, cloudy or concentrated, this is a sign of illness or overtraining). Try to have at least one nap and eat several small, nourishing meals. The following day, if you're still just as tired, you may be coming down with something; don't do anything except a long warmup; then rest.

Cure for Overtraining

The cure for overtraining is "Rest and Refueling," our equivalent of the military R and R.

Easy workouts can relieve the stiffness that often accompanies a layoff after training too hard. A 10-minute warmup and rolldown may make you feel better.

When you've recovered and have resumed training, *easy does it!* Don't try to make up for lost time. Very gradually increase the time, intensity and frequency of your workouts. Keep checking yourself on the measures of overtraining.

With indoor cycling, as with anything else, you can definitely have too much of a good thing. Exercise is supposed to make you feel good, fresh and shiny and full of energy. When it no longer does that, it's time to ease off for a while.

CHRONIC AND ACUTE FATIGUE

"Ranking today as one of the most frequently voiced of all complaints, chronic tiredness can stem from illness. But in many people, investigators report, it is the result of gradual deterioration of the body for lack of enough vigorous physical activity." Dr. Per-Olaf Astrand.

Chronic Fatigue

"I feel tired all the time, Doctor."

This is the most common complaint that doctors hear, usually followed by a long list of symptoms, any of which might be indications of organic disease—and are, 15% to 20% of the time.

Sometimes a slight illness is diagnosed, but it is not enough to account for the pervasive feeling of depression.

Chronic fatigue has the same effect as prolonged bedrest; it lessens your endurance. Something you formerly could do easily now leaves you breathless and with your heart pounding.

When you are dragging yourself through life, just making it through the day, and work is exhausting, the last thing you want to hear is that you should get more exercise.

All you want to do is sleep.

People who care about you cautiously suggest that you get more fresh air, meet new people, develop new interests, get out and *do* something.

All this should tell you that you are bored with life, but all you can feel is your exhaustion.

Pop psychologists may suggest that you hate your life and are running away from facing tensions—at home and/or at work. This may or may not be true.

It may just be that your physical activity level is so low that it's two steps away from bedrest.

Acute Fatigue

Busy people who get a lot done can push themselves over the limit by adding exercise to an already loaded schedule. Instead of feeling better they start feeling worse. And, if they go on a diet at the same time, they're really asking for trouble.

What they need is rest and refueling.

That's the R and R test that doctors use to tell acute fatigue from chronic fatigue.

If you feel better after a couple of days of taking it easy and fairly constant nibbling, you've been suffering from acute fatigue. If you still feel lousy, it's chronic.

Dr. Marion F. Graham, in his excellent book, *Inner Energy: How to Overcome Fatigue,* quotes a doctor, "I believe the world is kept turning by tired people. Maybe that's why they're so tired."

Allow yourself to rest, forget your diet for a while (a lot of small meals are best) and in a couple of days you'll feel almost as good as new.

Go-Getters… If you are always on the edge of overdoing it, aerobic training can push you over your limit. For, wonderful as exercise is for the sedentary, it can hurt the active. What seemed easy to do suddenly becomes very difficult.

Beginners… If you are starting to feel better from a program of aerobic exercise you can get so carried away that you ignore signals of tiredness. You work just as hard (at the same high level) even if you had trouble falling asleep the night before, even if your legs still hurt from the last workout, and even if your resting pulse rate has started to rise.

Success can cause failure… Watch out for the point where you're beginning to feel the training effect. You're doing great, you feel fit and strong, your speed and wind have improved. Your weight has dropped. You feel as if you could do anything —and you try. Suddenly you double the time or speed or resistance of your workout. Or you do all the regular stuff and add a 20-mile hike, a 3-mile walk, a 30-mile bike ride or three sets of tennis. Hard as it is to believe, one day of this can leave you wrecked for a week. Or longer.

In curing the disease, you have caused another version of it. Except for bruised muscles, it is hard to tell overtraining from chronic fatigue.

But the cure is very different.

MEDICAL ALERT

Never Cycle If You Have:
- Just had a heart attack
- Myocarditis (an inflamed heart muscle)
- Hepatitis
- Mononucleosis
- Acute phlebitis (blood clots in the veins)
- Any acute illness

Consult Your Doctor If You Have:
- Acute tuberculosis
- Asthma or other severe allergies
- Arthritis, because it can flare up (but moderate indoor cycling can increase your mobility)
- Gastrointestinal problems like colitis, ileitis or Crohn's disease
- Badly controlled diabetes
- Badly controlled hypertension (Blood pressure drops sharply right after exercise; this, combined with medication, may make it go too low.)
- Irregular heart rhythm (If you have a history of irregular heart rhythms at rest, during or after exercise, this may be one of the reasons your doctor suggests you take a stress test.)

Warning Signs

During or Right After Exercise (or Any Time, for That Matter):
- Dizziness
- Burst of irregular heartbeats
- Pulse dropping or becoming very low
- Chest pains or pressure in arm, shoulder or jaw or chest
- A feeling of indigestion

"Chest, neck or shoulder pain that appears during or after a workout is an indication to see a physician. If the pain disappears within five minutes, an individual should schedule an appointment before the next workout. If the pain lasts longer or is quite intense, immediate medical attention is warranted," according to Dr. Robert E. Bond, long-time cyclist and medical columnist for *Bicycle USA*.

Health Signals and What to Do About Them:

Most of these are caused by working at too high an intensity for your level of fitness. However, the temporary relief of symptoms and continuation of the program might mask or intensify an existing problem.
- Rapid heart action near training zone; pulse still high five minutes after workout
- Still breathing hard after ten minutes
- Stitch in side (Concentrate on pushing air out of the lungs and let the inhalation come naturally. Or draw in the diaphragm and breathe from chest. Repeated stitches in side may be an indication of a heart condition.)
- Vomiting and nausea (Besides working out at less effort, don't eat just before strenuous exercise. Racers advise waiting three hours.)
- Fatigue or insomnia (You may be training too hard.)
- Return of joint or arthritic pains (Rest until flare-up subsides. Check "Bike Fit" section again carefully. Try again at a lower level of intensity.)
- Cramp in muscle (Push thumb hard into middle of muscle.)

If These Home Remedies Don't Give Relief, See a Doctor.